The Triumphant Queen of the World

On Pilgrimage to Russia and China

The Triumphant Queen of the World

On Pilgrimage to Russia and China

DANIEL J. LYNCH

The Missionary Image of Our Lady of Guadalupe, Inc.
26 Lake Street
St. Albans, Vermont 05478

Copyright © 1995 Daniel J. Lynch

All rights reserved. This book may not be published or in any way reproduced in whole or in part, stored in a retrieval system, or transmitted, in any form or by any means, electronic, mechanical, photocopying, recording, or otherwise, without the written permission of the author whose address is:

26 Lake Street
St. Albans, Vermont 05478

Please do not copy without such permission.

Library of Congress Catalog Card No.: 95-78665

ISBN 0-9647988-2-4

Published by:

> The Missionary Image of Our Lady of Guadalupe, Inc.
> 26 Lake Street
> St. Albans, Vermont 05478

Printed in the United States of America

Dedication

This book is dedicated to Dr. Rosalie A. Turton of Washington, New Jersey. She is the founder of the 101 Foundation and was the courageous organizer of the Victorious Queen of the World Peace Flights 101 and 333 which carried almost 1000 pilgrims to Russia in 1992. She was also the organizer of the Triumphant Queen of the World Peace Flight 101 which carried almost 500 pilgrims to China in 1994. Both pilgrimages were accompanied by the Pilgrim Virgin statue of Our Lady of Fatima, the Missionary Image of Our Lady of Guadalupe and the Image of Jesus King of All Nations.

They said that it couldn't be done but Dr. Turton ignored all of the naysayers and overcame almost impossible odds to successfully organize these pilgrimages. She risked losing hundreds of thousands of dollars in chartering 747 airplanes, not seeing but believing that they would be filled with pilgrims.

"Blessed are those who have not seen yet have believed." Jn 20:29.

Dr. Rosalie A. Turton standing next to a demonic Chinese statue at the entrance to the Forbidden City. Dr. Turton is showing her Chinese Miraculous Medal with the Triumphant Queen of the World crushing the head of Satan.

Acknowledgments

I acknowledge and thank Lawrence Galloway, for many of his photographs which he has graciously given me permission to use.

I also acknowledge and thank Edward Norse, for some of his poems which he has graciously given me permission to use.

Contents

Introduction ix

Chapters

Part One
BEGINNINGS

1. The Fatima Message 1
2. The Akita Message 7
3. The Conversion of Russia 11
4. The 1992 Victorious Queen of the World
   Peace Flight 101 13
5. The Goal of China 29

Part Two
THE PILGRIMAGE TO CHINA

6. The Meaning of Pilgrimage 31
7. Our Lady's Army 33
8. The Statue and Images 37
9. Fatima, Portugal 41
10. Holy Land, Israel 43
11. Manila, Philippines 57
12. Shanghai and Beijing, China 69
13. Akita, Japan. 89

Part Three
WAR ON THE FAMILY

14. The Year of the Family 91
15. The Attack on the Family 95
16. The Myth of a Population Crisis 103
17. China: A Case Study of Population Control 105
18. The Counterattack by Spiritual Warfare 109
19. The Counterattack by
    The International Holy Family Year Congress 115

Contents

Part Four
THE FINAL DOGMA
20. The Alliance of the Two Hearts 119
21. Mary, Mediatrix of All Graces 123

Part Five
THE TRIUMPHANT QUEEN OF PEACE
22. Warnings and Chastisements 127
23. The Triumph of the Immaculate Heart of Mary and the Era of Peace 131
24. The New Evangelization and the Great Jubilee Year 2000 135
25. Epilogue: The Homecoming 139

Appendices
A. The Fatima Messages 143
B. The Fatima Prayers 145
C. The Akita Messages and Prayer 147
D. The Amsterdam Message and Prayer 149
E. St. Louis' Act of Total Consecration 151
F. Pope John Paul II's Act of Consecration of the World.... 153
G. Consecration to Mary Mediatrix of All Graces from the Jesus King of All Nations Devotion 157

Introduction

This book proclaims Our Lady as the Triumphant Queen of the World. She promised at Fatima, Portugal the triumph of her Immaculate Heart and the conversion of Russia. The beginning of the fulfillment of these promises is shown through the stories of Our Lady's pilgrimages to Russia and China by means of the Pilgrim Virgin statue of Our Lady of Fatima and the Missionary Image of Our Lady of Guadalupe. In 1992 they accompanied almost 1000 pilgrims on the Victorious Queen of the World Peace Flights 101 and 333 from Fatima through Europe to Russia. In 1994 they accompanied almost 500 pilgrims on the Triumphant Queen of the World Peace Flight 101 from Fatima around the world to China.

The pilgrims journeyed to the sites of some of Our Lady's greatest spiritual victories over hearts and minds particularly in Fatima, Portugal; Lourdes and Paris, France; Manila, Philippines; Moscow, Russia; and to the place of her coming great victory in Beijing, China.

You will learn the historical background and significance of these sites and those of the Holy Land.

The book explains the messages and requests of Our Lady at Fatima, Akita, Lipa, and Amsterdam. It demonstrates how they are all linked with each other and with the messages of the Jesus King of All Nations Devotion towards the proclamation of the Final Marian Dogma that Our Lady is the Mediatrix of All Graces.

The 1994 pilgrimage occurred during the Year of the Family. The attack on the family is detailed together with the Holy Father's counterattack by spiritual warfare with Our Lady and St. Michael the Archangel and the counterattack by the International Holy Family Year Congress Resolutions which promote the devotion of the Alliance of the Two Hearts and Our Lady's requests made at Fatima and Akita.

The myth of a "Population Crisis" is destroyed and a case study is made of population control in China by forced sterilizations and abortions.

The persecution of the Church in China, as prophesied by Our Lady at Fatima, is detailed together with the Holy Father's benevolent pastoral attitude to Catholics who belong to the government-controlled Patriotic Catholic Association.

Great hope is left for the future by reason of the Holy Father's proclamation of the Great Jubilee of the Year 2000 which will be, as he said, "the great meeting with God's merciful love that awaits us at the beginning of the third Christian millennium."

PART ONE

Beginnings

1. The Fatima Message

On May 13, 1917, in the twilight before the darkness of the Communist Revolution in Russia, the Blessed Virgin Mary intervened in human history and brought one of the greatest miracles of all time. She appeared to three shepherd children at Fatima, Portugal and identified herself as the "Lady of the Rosary."

She requested that we amend our lives and ask pardon for our sins, pray and sacrifice for sinners and recite the daily Rosary to bring peace to the world. She said that if men did not stop offending God, another war would begin that would be more terrible than the First World War which was then raging. She said that war is a punishment from God for sins and that this new chastisement from God would be signalled by a night illumined by an unknown light.

To our horror, this prophecy was fulfilled 21 years later. On January 25, 1938 this unknown light appeared over the northern horizon and was seen all over the world. Forty-five days later, Hitler invaded Austria and started World War II which claimed thirty five million lives.

Our Lady of Fatima also requested that Russia be consecrated to her Immaculate Heart and that we receive Holy Communions of reparation on the first Saturday of each month. She added that if her requests were not fulfilled, Russia would spread her errors throughout the world bringing new wars and persecutions of the Church; the good would be martyred; the Holy Father would have much to suffer and certain nations would be annihilated. This prophecy was also fulfilled except for the annihilation of nations, which may yet be fulfilled if we do not heed her requests.

However, she promised that in the end her Immaculate Heart would triumph; the Holy Father would consecrate Russia to her Immaculate Heart; Russia would be converted and the world would enjoy a period of peace.

Our Lady also prophesied the exact time and date of a public miracle in order that all might believe her messages. This miracle occurred at noon on October 13, 1917. Over 70,000 people witnessed a ball of fire, that seemed to be the sun, spin like a pinwheel in the sky, change colors and plunge towards the earth. Just as the terrified people thought that the world was at its end, the ball of fire returned to the sun in its normal place in the sky.

This miracle is one of the greatest miracles in the history of the world. It immediately dried up a lake of water and mud in rain-swept Fatima and was seen up to 32 miles away. Even its heat was felt by the witnesses. This should give us all the more reason to respond to Our Lady's messages.

On June 13, 1917, Our Lady appeared at Fatima holding her Immaculate Heart out from her body in her left hand. It was vertically encircled by thorns which represent the offensive sins of humanity. She told Sister Lucia, one of the visionaries who was still living in 1995, "Jesus wants to use you to make me known and loved, He wants to establish in the world devotion to my Immaculate Heart. To those who embrace it I promise salvation." Jesus later told Sister Lucia, "Have compassion on the heart of your most holy Mother, covered with thorns, with which ungrateful men pierce it at every moment, and there is no one to make an act of reparation to remove them."

This devotion or consecration to the Immaculate Heart of Mary, with its extraordinary promise of salvation, and our reparation to her for the sins of the world is the essential message of Fatima. This message is in union with the request for consecration and reparation to the Sacred Heart of Jesus which was explained by Pope Pius XI in his encyclical, *Miserentissimus Redemptor*, as follows,

> Whereas the primary object of consecration is that the creature should repay the love of the Creator by loving Him in return, yet from this another naturally follows - that is to make amends for the insults offered to the Divine Love by oblivion and neglect, and by the sins and offenses of mankind. This duty is commonly called by the name of 'reparation'.

"Reparation" means to repair or to make up for the sins of others. Jesus is our only Redeemer because He alone is the mediator between God and men and made full reparation for our sins. Heb 9:15; 1 Tim 2:5. This is known as the Objective Redemption.

Jesus' reparative self-offering is evidenced in the Prayer of Reparation taught by the Angel to the children of Fatima,

> O most Holy Trinity, Father, Son and Holy Spirit, I adore Thee profoundly. I offer Thee the most precious Body, Blood, Soul and Divinity of Jesus Christ, present in all the tabernacles of the world, in reparation for the outrages, sacrileges and indifference by which He is offended. By the infinite merits of the Sacred Heart of Jesus and the Immaculate Heart of Mary, I beg the conversion of poor sinners.

In His great love, Jesus has willed to take into partnership in His redemptive work all of us whom He redeemed in order that the merciful work of His love may shine forth through us. This merciful work of love is shared by all of us who in reparation make sacrifices and unite our sufferings with Christ. This is what Saint Paul meant when he said, "In my own flesh I fill up what is lacking in the sufferings of Christ for the sake of His body, the Church." Col 1:24.

If one part of a body is weak, such as a paralyzed arm, the other arm must work harder to make up for the weakness. So it is with the Mystical Body of Christ, the Church. If one member is weak through sin, another must make up for him. This is known as the Subjective Redemption.

Our Lady encouraged us to take part in this merciful work of love at Fatima when she said, "Pray, pray very much, and make sacrifices for sinners; for many souls go to hell, because there are none to sacrifice themselves and to pray for them."

Pope John Paul II summarized the Fatima call to consecration and reparation on April 12, 1985 when he said that we must collaborate "with Christ the Redeemer through the offering of [our] own lives united and lived with the Heart of Christ in total consecration to His love and in reparation for the sins of the world, through the Immaculate Heart of Mary Most Holy."

Our personal program of consecration is to live our Baptismal promises to renounce Satan and to offer ourselves totally to Jesus Christ. We can do this by following Pope John Paul II's example and renewing our Baptismal promises through making the Total Consecration formula of St. Louis de Montfort. This formula is contained in the Appendices.

Our personal program of reparation is to make Our Lady's requested Communion of Reparation on First Saturdays by receiving Confession and Holy Communion, reciting the Rosary, and meditating for fifteen minutes on the mysteries all with the intention of making reparation to her Immaculate Heart. To this we should add adoration of the Blessed Sacrament and the daily offering of all of our prayers, works, joys and sufferings.

Our Lady told Sister Lucia that for those who practice the First Saturday Communion of Reparation for five months in a row, "I promise to assist them in the hour of their death with all the necessary graces for salvation." Our Lady's promise of salvation through consecration and reparation to her Immaculate Heart is a tremendous grace which should motivate us to respond to her requests.

Beginnings

The Immaculate Heart of Mary as she appeared to the children at Fatima and requested the establishment of devotion in the world to her Immaculate Heart.

Stained glass window of the angel as he appeared to the children at Fatima and revealed the Prayer of Reparation.

2. The Akita Message

On July 6, 1973, Our Lady appeared from a statue of Our Lady of All Nations to Sister Agnes Sasagawa of the Handmaids of the Eucharist in Akita, Japan. The apparitions were declared authentic by the local Bishop, John Ito, with the approval of Cardinal Joseph Ratzinger, President Prefect of the Congregation for the Doctrine of the Faith. Bishop Ito affirmed that the messages of Fatima and Akita are essentially the same.

As at Fatima, consecration, reparation and the real presence of Jesus in the Blessed Sacrament were emphasized. Sister Agnes was accustomed to recite a Eucharistic Prayer similar to the Prayer of Reparation that the Angel taught the Fatima children. Our Lady told Sister Agnes to add the word "truly" as capitalized in the following Eucharistic Prayer which she recited,

> Most Sacred Heart of Jesus, TRULY present in the Holy Eucharist, I consecrate my body and soul to be entirely one with Your Heart, being sacrificed at every instant on all the altars of the world and giving praise to the Father, pleading for the coming of His Kingdom.
>
> Please receive this humble offering of myself. Use me as You will for the glory of the Father and the salvation of souls. Most Holy Mother of God, never let me be separated from Your Divine Son. Please defend and protect me as Your special child. Amen.

On August 6, Our Lady appeared to Sister Agnes with a message pleading for reparation and warning of a great chastisement, she said,

> Many people in this world afflict the Lord. I desire souls to console Him to soften the anger of the Heavenly Father. I wish, with my Son, for souls who will make reparation by their suffering and their poverty for the sinners and the ungrateful.
>
> In order that the world might know His anger, the Heavenly Father is preparing to inflict a great chastisement on all mankind. With my Son I have intervened so many times to appease the wrath of the Father. I have prevented the coming of calamities by offering Him the sufferings of the Son on the Cross, His Precious Blood, and beloved souls who console Him, forming a cohort of victim souls. Prayer, penance and courageous sacrifices can soften the Father's anger. I desire this also from your community; that it love poverty, that it sanctify itself and pray in reparation for the ingratitude and outrages of so many men. Recite the prayer of the Handmaids of the Eucharist with awareness of its meaning; put it into practice; offer in reparation [whatever God may allow] for sins. Let each one endeavor, according to capacity and position, to offer herself entirely to the Lord.

Bishop Ito said, "It seems to me that Our Heavenly Father needs to purify this corrupt world before allowing mankind to enter the 21st century. The Blessed Mother appears to ask for souls who will offer up their fervent prayers, sacrifices, and sufferings to God in order to contribute to the realization of God's Kingdom of Justice and Love."

Sister Agnes herself offered the sacrifices and sufferings of her temporary deafness and a gravely painful cross-shaped wound in her left hand which matched a cross-shaped wound in the right hand of the Akita statue of Our Lady of All Nations. Both the wound on Sister Agnes and the wound on the statue bled.

The messages to Sister Agnes were received amidst many other supernatural happenings including perspiration of the statue which exuded a sweet perfume. From January 4, 1975 until

September 15, 1981, the statue cried miraculous tears 101 times. Scientific examination proved that these were human tears.

Bishop Ito said that he thought that the statue wept because of Our Lady's statement, "The thought of the loss of so many souls is the cause of my sadness."

On the evening of the first day of the miraculous tears the Angel explained the meaning of Our Lady's tears to Sister Agnes. The Angel said, "She weeps because she wishes the conversion of the greatest number. She desires that souls be consecrated to Jesus and to the Father by her intercession."

On May 1, 1976, First Saturday, the Angel said, "Attach great importance to this day for the glory of God and of His Holy Mother. With courage spread this devotion (the Fatima First Saturday Devotion) among the greatest number."

Two weeks after the end of the miraculous tears, Sr. Agnes had a vision of a large, majestic Bible and the Angel instructed her to read the passage before her eyes. It said, "I will place enmity between you (Satan) and the Woman (Mary) and between your seed and hers (Jesus). She will crush your head and you shall lie in wait for her heel." Gn 3:15.

The Angel then told Sister Agnes the reason that the statue wept 101 times. The angel said, "There is a meaning to the figure one hundred and one. This signifies that sin came into the world by a woman and it is also by a woman that salvation came to the world. The '0' between the two 'ones' signifies the Eternal God who is from all eternity until eternity. The first '1' represents Eve and the last '1' the Virgin Mary."

This revelation was the basis for the name of the 101 Foundation, organizer of the Victorious Queen of the World Peace Flight 101 to Russia in 1992 and the Triumphant Queen of the World Peace Flight 101 to China in 1994.

10   *Beginnings*

The weeping statue of Our Lady at Akita, Japan.

Akita visionary, Sister Agnes Sasagawa.

The Pilgrim Virgin statue, Bishop John Ito, Doctor Rosalie Turton and the statue of Our Lady of Akita.

3. The Conversion of Russia

On July 13, 1917, Our Lady of Fatima told Sister Lucia, "The Holy Father will consecrate Russia to me and she will be converted." This consecration took place on March 25, 1984 at St. Peter's Square in Rome by Pope John Paul II collegially in union with the Bishops of the world.

The Holy Father consecrated the world to the Immaculate Heart of Mary before a quarter million of the faithful and the original statue of Our Lady of Fatima which had been brought to Rome from the Fatima Shrine. This Collegial Consecration prayer is contained in the Appendices.

The Collegial Consecration had its roots in the consecration of Poland and in various consecrations made by the popes since Pope Pius XII. However, none of these were in union with the Bishops of the world.

On December 8, 1953, after a three week retreat, Cardinal Wysznski of Poland consecrated himself to Jesus through Mary according to the Total Consecration formula of St. Louis de Montfort. In 1956 he ordered that the whole country be consecrated to Our Lady at the National Shrine of Czestochowa.

In 1978 Polish Cardinal Karol Wojtyla, who had made St. Louis' Total Consecration, became Pope John Paul II and Lech Walesa who had made the same consecration founded the Polish workers' Independent Solidarity Union.

Beginnings

Shortly before Cardinal Wysznski's death, Father René Laurentin asked him for an explanation of Poland's great non-violent victories over Communism. The aged Cardinal picked up St. Louis de Montfort's *True Devotion to Mary*, showed it to Father Laurentin and said, "But it was the Blessed Virgin!"

And it was the Blessed Virgin who continued these victories in Eastern Europe after Pope John Paul II's Collegial Consecration of 1984. In March 1985 Mikhail Gorbachev became the leader of the Soviet Union. In 1990 he made an unprecedented visit to Pope John Paul II and asked him to pray for him and his country. As the forces of Communism dissipated, a last struggle was made to maintain it through a coup attempt against Gorbachev which was defeated on August 22, 1991, the Feast of the Queenship of Mary.

On that same day, Latvia and Estonia became independent nations. On Christmas Day 1991, seven years after the Holy Father's Collegial Consecration, the Soviet flag was brought down from the Kremlin. Gorbachev said that these remarkable events "would not have been possible without the presence of this Pope."

Sister Lucia confirmed that the Collegial Consecration made by Pope John Paul II was accepted by Our Lady as a fulfillment of her request made at Fatima even though it did not mention the word "Russia". The Holy Father's consecration, she said, "prevented a nuclear war that would have occurred in 1985."

Sister Lucia also said that the meaning of the phrase "the conversion of Russia" meant the liberation of Russia from militant atheistic Communism which had prevented the Russian people from practicing their faith. They are now free to do so.

Sister Lucia
with Pope John Paul II.

Pope John Paul II's Collegial Consecration
of the world to the
Immaculate Heart of Mary.

4. The 1992 Victorious Queen of the World Peace Flight 101

The largest airborne pilgrimage in the world travelled to Russia to proclaim Our Lady as Queen of Russia and to pray for unity of the Catholic and the Orthodox Churches. Dr. Rosalie Turton of the 101 Foundation organized the Victorious Queen of the World Peace Flight 101 consisting of 940 pilgrims including 60 priests, 6 Bishops, several mystics and the author on two Boeing 747 airplanes. John Haffert, co-founder of the Blue Army (The World Apostolate of Fatima), was also a leader. The pilgrimage occurred in October of 1992 during the 75th anniversaries of the apparitions of Our Lady of Fatima and the Communist Revolution in Russia.

Shortly before we left on our pilgrimage, Our Lady appeared in Alaska to one of the visionaries of the Jesus King of All Nations Devotion. She said, "My daughter, I want to talk about my daughter Russia. She has been dead for all spiritual purposes. Only the cells of a scattered few have remained faithful. Because of the world's prayers for her conversion, I have resurrected my daughter, Russia, she is no longer dead but asleep. Underneath her now are the glowing embers of the spiritual life."

Then Our Lord appeared to her as a warrior with a tremendous bow and a quiver with many arrows. He said, "This bow represents the prayers of all of the people who prayed for the conversion of Russia for all of these years. The arrows are like the pilgrims that I am sending to Russia and the other lands carrying the fire of my love like the flints of my arrowheads."

Jesus then shot arrows across the waters from Alaska to Russia and they ignited in flames when they hit. Flames of the love of God exploded from dormant embers and came to life in Russia and all of the surrounding countries as well, as if in a huge forest backfire.

Our pilgrimage was led by the International Pilgrim Virgin Statue of Our Lady of Fatima, the Missionary Image of Our Lady of Guadalupe and the Image of Jesus King of All Nations both of which are six feet tall.

The Pilgrim Virgin statue began its world journey in 1947 when a World Youth Congress at Fatima resolved that it should be carried publicly to Russia. Pope Pius XII referred to the statue as "The Queen of the World" and later in his encyclical *Ad Caeli Reginam* said that it travelled as "the messenger of the royalty of Mary."

On October 7, 1992, Feast of the Holy Rosary, 45 years after the beginning of its journey to the nations, Our Lady's statue left for Paris, France as the messenger of her royalty began the pilgrimage to Russia with the images of Our Lady of Guadalupe and Jesus King of All Nations. We pilgrims carried the statue and images together with the prayers and sacrifices of millions over those years with us.

We celebrated our first Mass in the largest church in Paris, St. Sulpice. Here before the huge statue of Mary, Queen of the World, St. Louis de Montfort said his first Mass. His book *True Devotion to Mary* teaches the Total Consecration to her which is the spirituality of Pope John Paul II.

We also celebrated Mass in the chapel at Rue du Bac in Paris where Our Lady appeared to St. Catherine Labouré in 1830 and revealed the Miraculous Medal devotion. Here Our Lady also appeared to St. Catherine standing on the world, crushing Satan and revealing her great victory prophesied in the Book of Genesis, chapter 3 verse 15.

In Paris we also visited the Church of Our Lady of Victories where in 1870 the pastor heard in prayer that France had been saved from defeat by the Germans in the Franco-Prussian War. He was told, "Tonight, between eight and nine o'clock, France has been saved by Our Lady of Victories."

At that very hour Our Lady appeared in the sky over the village of Pontmain. While the startled villagers prayed the Rosary, there appeared at Our Lady's feet the words, "But pray, my children, my Son permits Himself to be moved by your prayers." At that very same hour the German general received inexplicable orders not to advance any farther in France. Nine days later at the conclusion of a novena of thanksgiving, the armistice was signed!

Also at this Church before the statue of Our Lady of Victories, St. Therese of Lisieux gave thanks for her cure from a deadly illness. Our Lady told her that it was indeed she who had cured her. I had brought a relic of St. Therese in a pyx and whenever I opened it for veneration of the pilgrims, it emitted a strong perfume of roses!

The Church of Our Lady of Victories had been consecrated to the Immaculate Heart of Mary in 1835. This resulted in many conversions and a great increase in Mass attendance. A confraternity was started here which was the first organized effort to promote consecration to the Immaculate Heart. As such, I led the pilgrims in praying St. Louis' Act of Total Consecration before we left.

As I did so, Our Lady appeared to one of our pilgrim doctors and said, "Go to my son (meaning me) and obtain from him this Act of Consecration and lead all of my pilgrims in this when you take them to my Church in Eastport, New York."

Before our pilgrimage, Our Lady had asked this doctor to lead a pilgrimage on her return home to the same named Church, Our Lady of Victories, in Eastport, New York. In obedience she organized this pilgrimage without knowing its purpose. Now she knew!

On October 13, 1992, the 75th anniversary of the last apparition of Fatima, the Missionary Image and the Image of Jesus King of All Nations were processed at Fatima with the original Fatima statue and were placed in the middle of the plaza which was filled with approximately three quarters of a million faithful.

Our Lady had prophesied through American visionary Janie Garza, a Filipino visionary and a priest, all of whom were on our pilgrimage, that she would send a dove as a sign for us to have confidence in her intercession for the success of our mission to Russia. To our amazement, after the Mass a dove came down from the sky and alighted above the left hand of the Image of Jesus King of All Nations while the pilgrims recited the Devotion's Chaplet of Unity. It reminded us of what John the Baptist said, "I saw the Spirit descend from the sky like a dove and remain upon Him." Jn 1:32.

The dove then turned, faced the pilgrims and walked back and forth on the Image bowing his head to them as if he were thanking them for their prayers. The dove stayed for several minutes amidst the joyful crying of the pilgrims who were jubilantly waving their handkerchiefs.

Another visionary reported that when the dove alighted, rays appeared from the Missionary Image glowing out in all directions onto the crowd and Our Lady was smiling from her Image upon all her people. The visionary said, "During the time that I was having this inner vision I think a bomb could have dropped in front of me and I would not have been able to move because the vision was so intense." The Filipino visionary also saw Our Lady of Guadalupe come from her Image in a bright light which proceeded from her to the crowd.

Our Lady then appeared to pilgrim Janie Garza from the midst of the Miracle of the Sun as a radiant person brighter than the sun. She said, "I am the Lady of Light and I will enlighten each one of you."

The priest, to whom Our Lady had prophesied the coming of the dove, came to the pilgrims around the images after the Mass to explain to them that a dove would come. To his happy surprise, the dove beat him to the images and Father said, "Everyone was filled with such great joy and tears and praise of God that it was like walking into the upper room on the day of Pentecost!"

The 1992 Victorious Queen of the World Peace Flight 101   17

"Victorious Queen Peace Flight" logo on pilgrimage airplane.

Statue of Our Lady, Queen of the World, St. Sulpice Church, Paris, France.

Almost 1,000 pilgrims gather in front of the Basilica at Lourdes, France.

Fatima, Portugal on the 75th anniversary of Our Lady's last apparition there, October 13, 1992, with the Missionary Image and the image of Jesus King of All Nations upon which a dove landed and remained as prophesied by three mystics.

Three days later, on our way to Russia, Our Lady of Guadalupe appeared to Janie Garza and said, "Do not have the smallest worry. You should only be concerned with being in a loving and prayerful spirit."

Our Lady told pilgrim visionary Estella Ruiz, "This journey is part of my plan to bring many souls to God. My heart rejoices as you, my instruments of peace, come with me to greet, with love and compassion, your sister, Russia, into our fold. This journey to Russia has dealt the evil one a great blow and this is indeed a glorious victory."

Our Lady told pilgrim locutionist Dorothy Romano, "As you enter Russia, I want you to know the danger that awaits all of you, but I will thwart the enemy who lies in wait." She told Irish pilgrim visionary Christina Gallagher, "Long have I cried to sow the rich seed of grace in the hearts of my children of Russia. Blessed are the peacemakers and all who strive for peace. With peace, there is unity and hope: All comes through love and Christ Jesus is LOVE."

We arrived in Moscow on October 16, the 75th anniversary of the founding of the Knights of the Immaculata by St. Maximilian Kolbe. While he was in Rome in 1917, the Freemasons celebrated their second centenary. They made Rome the center of their sacrilegious demonstrations. They marched to St. Peter's where they displayed their blasphemous banners. One said, "Satan must reign in the Vatican. The Pope will be his slave."

This inspired St. Maximilian to found the Knights in order, as he said, "to build a trench and personally hurl back the assaults of the foe." He revised the prayer of the Miraculous Medal to say, "O Mary conceived without sin, pray for us who have recourse to you and for those who have no recourse to you, especially the Freemasons."

St. Maximilian prophesied, "One day, you will see the statue of the Immaculata in the center of Moscow atop the Kremlin!" Now we were fulfilling this prophecy as we brought the statue of the Immaculata to the center of Moscow.

Our Lady told Estella Ruiz, "As you move on to the final events, you must know and understand that they are really a beginning of other significant events that will allow the world to see the great love with which my Immaculate Heart will triumph! Now, open your hearts and arms to your brothers and sisters in Russia, showing them the love of God, letting them know that Our Lord never forgot them or abandoned them. Spread throughout your love and mine by means of the gifts you have brought and let them know that God lives in the world and wants to show them His love through you."

As we entered Moscow, our tour guide said that she was happy to welcome us to the city and pleased to say that it was now the capital of *Russia* and no longer of the Soviet Union. She said, "Although we had 73 years of atheism and were brought up as atheists, yet we were born with the love of God in our hearts, and we really are true Christians and we welcome you to pray with us. I welcome you with an open heart and tears in my eyes and we thank you for coming. Like the universe we are not separated anymore. We are not closed anymore. We are allowed to tell you what we feel and we are happy about this so that when you come here to share with us all of our troubles you can join us in looking to the future with optimism. Because as long as you are with us and we are all together as children of God, it makes us happy.

"Our young people have no morals," she continued, "because they were brought up through atheistic Communism and there was no model of goodness for them. There were no parents, no teachers, no persons to tell them the difference between right and wrong. There was no one. But now they must learn that even if there is no one, they are not alone here and that there is always God with them who loves them and who will help them to do good. Thank you for praying for Russia. This is what we need. You have brought love to this country, you have brought us God. Thank you."

We distributed six tons of religious goods and thousands of holy cards and Rosaries all of which were gratefully received by the Russian people who often broke down in tears. None were thrown to the ground as so often happens elsewhere.

On October 18, as we approached Red Square in Moscow on our bus, I led the Visitation mystery of the Rosary. As I meditated, I told the pilgrims that I was sorry that we had not planned a big pageant for Our Lady to triumphantly enter Red Square like

Jesus entered Jerusalem to the waving of palm leaves and the sounds of "Hosannahs". "Then again," I said, "it's the little unplanned things that hit our Mother's heart such as when a six year old gives a scribbly birthday card to her mother, as compared to when a 21 year old gives an embroidered tablecloth. So let's just offer our Mother our scribbles today as her little children in her motley army."

As we reached Red Square, we got the Missionary Image and the Image of Jesus King of All Nations out from the bus together with a large crucifix and, as we sang "Onward Christian Soldiers", as Our Lady had requested, I led a procession to the edge of Red Square which was barricaded. We waited for the arrival of the Pilgrim Virgin statue outside the barricades in front of the site of the former Cathedral of Our Lady of Kazan, which had been destroyed by Stalin.

As I looked across the immense plaza of Red Square, I could see some of our blue-coated pilgrims on the other side. Father John Hoke said that the Pilgrim Virgin statue was across the Square and he opened the barricades a little bit. I told the pilgrims to follow me and to break through the barricades as I led the images with the crucifix across Red Square and approached the other side. The Russian police were astonished that we passed the barricades but Father John calmed their fears and they let us proceed.

Many of the pilgrims saw the Pilgrim Virgin statue on the other side of the Square being carried high above the heads of the people gathered there. So we processed towards her. In fact, what we saw was a *vision* of the statue and not the statue itself, which never entered Red Square that morning. Our Lady used this vision to draw me and the pilgrims across the entire length of Red Square towards St. Basil's Cathedral on the other side. As I approached St. Basil's, the vision disappeared and I had no idea where to go!

I looked out of the corner of my eye and I saw a circular platform monument with nine concrete steps. I literally ran to the top of these steps urging everyone to follow me and to surround me and the images so that the police would not arrest us. I planted the crucifix at the top of the platform in a manner reminiscent of the Marines planting the flag on the top of Mt. Surabachi on Iwo Jima.

The 1992 Victorious Queen of the World Peace Flight 101

Here I proclaimed Our Lady as Queen of Russia and of All Nations and Jesus as King of Russia and All Nations. I said that we were there to claim the country of Russia for the Immaculate Heart of Mary and Christ the King. I said, "When the Holy Father consecrated the world to the Immaculate Heart of Mary in 1984, Sister Lucia said that God will keep His promise, meaning that Russia will be converted." I continued, "The conversion of Russia will ignite the Divine Flame of the love of God which will proceed from Russia throughout the entire world and set the whole world on fire for Christ so that Jesus Christ will be truly King of All Nations and will reign in all hearts."

John Haffert was standing next to me and I handed him a tiny crown from a small statue of Our Lady of Fatima. I announced that Our Lady was so humble that she came in this small statue, rather than the International Pilgrim Virgin statue. I said to John, "In honor of your forty plus years of service to Our Lady please crown her as Queen of Russia." He did so.

At that moment, Janie Garza said that Red Square lit up like the Fourth of July in a vision that she had. Our Lady appeared to her and said that she was very pleased and happy with all of our efforts and troubles. She appeared as Our Lady of Fatima over Red Square wearing a crown. Light streamed from her heart flooding the Square and bounced up and outward in all directions. She said, "Thank you for your obedience and prayers. You, my children, have overcome many obstacles by obedience and prayer. You have brought so much joy to my heart. Know that your rewards are great in heaven for you have pleased God. Remain small in the eyes of the world so that you may be great in the eyes of God.

"Your sister Russia, my children, needs your love and faith. My children, I too am embracing my children in Russia. Let us go together and embrace her with God's love."

Later, our tour guide told me that she was astonished that we were able to process into Red Square without being stopped by the police. She added that the spot from which I proclaimed the Queenship and Kingship of Mary and Jesus was a monument from which the Tsars used to proclaim their edicts to the Russian peoples! She also said that I made the proclamation in front of

Spasskey Tower on the Kremlin Wall which means "Savior's Tower".

From Red Square we proceeded to the Cathedral of the Patriarch of the Russian Orthodox Church to be received by the Metropolitan of Moscow as the Patriarch's representative. The day before was the feast of Our Lady's Intercession, one of the greatest feasts of the Orthodox Church. Our Lady interceded for us and provided an audience for pilgrim Father Ken Roberts with the Patriarch. Father Ken explained the mission of our Peace Flight to the Patriarch and expressed his hope to present him with an icon of Our Lady of Fatima.

In a wonderful ecumenical move, the Patriarch designated the Metropolitan as his representative to receive the icon and us in his Cathedral the next day. Remarkably, for the first time in history, the Patriarch was allowing prayer for reconciliation and unity between the Catholic and the Orthodox Churches. Moreover, this was to occur in his Cathedral publicly in front of a congregation after celebration of the divine liturgy.

We arrived at the Cathedral to find it packed with at least a thousand standing worshippers singing melodious Russian hymns. The whole Cathedral was sparkling in gold with hundreds of burning candles, beautiful icons on every wall and column and the smell of incense rising to the ceiling. We were escorted to the very front left of the altar.

The Metropolitan was clothed in magnificent golden vestments and wore a gold crown just like the image of Jesus King of All Nations. He began preaching to his congregation, "It is our own fault that we suffered from Communism. We didn't pray enough and allowed bad leaders to govern us. Now we must admit that we are sinners and turn back to God. We have a great task to accomplish."

Father Ken held the icon of Our Lady of Fatima in front of his chest. After the liturgy the Metropolitan approached him and Father Ken gave him the icon. The Metropolitan accepted it in the name of the Patriarch, recognized Our Lady and said, "Our Lady of Fatima, we know her and ask her to bring us peace. We thank the Blue Army and all who have prayed for Russia."

Turning to his congregation he said, "We knew of the message of Fatima and during our dark years her message was our hope."

Then Father Ken explained that we came to pray for the unity of the Catholic and the Orthodox Churches. The Metropolitan agreed and said, "I will pray for unity and if you agree with my prayer, say 'Amen'. Then you will pray for unity and if I agree with your prayer, I will say 'Amen'." With that understanding each of them prayed before the replica icon of Our Lady of Kazan, from the grounds of whose destroyed Cathedral we had just come. Each said 'Amen' to each other's prayer to the joy of the pilgrims and the congregation.

Then the Metropolitan gave each of us a small icon of Our Lady of Kazan to keep as a remembrance of this historic occasion after nearly 1000 years of division. We all left the Cathedral filled with joyful hope.

During this historic day, 45 years after the World Youth Congress which launched the world-wide pilgrimage of the Pilgrim Virgin Statue, another World Youth Congress was taking place in Moscow. It seemed that Our Lady didn't enter Red Square by that statue that morning out of consideration and respect for these youth who were busy that morning passing resolutions to respond to the requests that she had made at Fatima.

So we decided to process the Pilgrim Virgin Statue into Red Square again that evening with the youth. It also seemed as if Our Lady had waited until her apostle of consecration, Bishop Paulo Hnilica, arrived from Fatima.

Around 11:30 p.m. we gathered outside Red Square on the opposite side from our gathering that morning. I entered the Square and scouted out the area and the police. There was only one police car parked near the Square and some soldiers guarding Lenin's tomb. I decided to lead the pilgrims to Lenin's tomb in reparation for his bringing of atheistic Communism to Russia and the millions of innocents that were killed because of it.

Again I carried the crucifix leading the pilgrims and the Pilgrim Virgin Statue across Red Square, this time from the opposite side. We sang hymns in the pouring rain as we processed to the tomb of Lenin. We stopped about ten yards in front of the tomb and its soldiers. We began to pray the Rosary and soon the tower clock struck midnight.

Bishop Hnilica then suggested that we interrupt the Rosary and crown Our Lady as Queen of Russia. A 14 year old Russian girl, who had just been baptized two weeks before, was chosen to crown her. As she crowned the statue, the soldiers changed their guard (as if symbolizing a change for Russia), a pink dawn appeared in the midnight sky (as if symbolizing a new day for Russia), and the rain miraculously stopped above us but continued around us as if we were in a dry eye of a rainstorm!

As Our Lady was crowned, Bishop Hnilica related a story. "On March 25, 1984 when the Holy Father asked the Bishops to collegially join him in the consecration of the world to the Immaculate Heart of Mary, I was here in the heart of the Kremlin in the Cathedral of the Annunciation. I clandestinely prayed the consecration prayer and as I left the Cathedral I saw a huge banner hanging over Red Square proclaiming, 'Communism Has Triumphed!'

"But now, eight years later, that banner is down!; the Soviet Union is down!; Communism is down!; Our Lady has been crowned as Queen of Russia and the Triumph of the Immaculate Heart of Mary has begun!"

This is how the conversion of Russia began through the end of the persecution of the Church in Russia which has enabled the Russians to be free to choose Christ.

Our Lady told Estella Ruiz, "I speak to the Peace Pilgrims whom I commissioned to take my love to my daughter, Russia, that she may know of my love for her through you. You have seen but a slight glimpse of the tremendous amount of pain that had engulfed my children under the evil siege of Communism. You found your days in the desert hard, but this was a small example of the constant pain in which your brothers and sisters under Communism have lived for so long.

"My beloved little ones, you must begin to understand the significance of the event you have been involved in. This event is the spark that ignited the fire that will become a blaze throughout the world of the love of my Immaculate Heart. It is through Russia's conversion that the world will know that these times are truly the reign of my heart and that my love for God and for my earthly children will triumph over evil, so that all nations will know and acknowledge that my Son, Our Lord, Jesus, is the King of the World and the Hope and Salvation of all."

To celebrate Russia's liberation from militant atheistic Communism, we had a Eucharistic Holy Hour of Adoration during our last night in Russia on an altar over an upside down statue of the head of Lenin.

The room that the hotel in St. Petersburg had scheduled for us at the end of our Russian visitation was the Communist Meeting Room. When I entered this room I noticed a large red Communist flag on a staff in one corner of the front, a 4 foot bust statue of Lenin on a pedestal in the other corner and a meeting table in the center.

I proceeded to the front of the room, rolled up the flag around its staff and laid it down on the floor. Then I picked up the statue of the head of Lenin, turned it upside down and placed it backwards under the meeting table which I set up for our altar. Father John then exposed the Blessed Sacrament on the altar.

I announced to the adorers that I had figuratively decapitated Lenin and set him beneath the feet of Christ who, through Our Lady's intercession, had crushed his head and that of Communism. I reminded them of the Old Testament story of Judith who courageously entered the enemy's camp and decapitated the head of their ruler, Holofernes.

I then read Judith 15:9-10 which relates the congratulations of the Israelites to their heroine, as we should congratulate Our Lady for conquering Communism,

> You are the glory of Jerusalem, the surpassing joy of Israel; you are the splendid boast of our people. With your own hand you have done all this; you have done good to Israel, and God is pleased with what you have wrought. May you be blessed by the Lord Almighty forever and ever! And all the people answered, Amen!

26 *Beginnings*

Author leading procession of pilgrims across Red Square.

John Haffert crowns small statue of Our Lady of Fatima in Red Square.

The 1992 Victorious Queen of the World Peace Flight 101   27

Author proclaiming Our Lady as Queen and Jesus as King of Russia and All Nations in Red Square after crowning of small statue of our Lady of Fatima by Blue Army founder John Haffert.

The icon of Our Lady of Fatima presented by Father Ken Roberts to the Metropolitan of Moscow.

28 *Beginnings*

Russian congregation witnessing prayers for unity of the Catholic and Orthodox Churches.

World Youth celebrating an International Congress in Moscow in honor of the Two Hearts.

Author "decapitating" Lenin and holding statue of his head upside down.

5. The Goal of China

Our Lady of Fatima said that if we did not repent and pray, "Russia will spread her errors throughout the world." This prophecy was fulfilled and Russian Communism spread throughout the world and particularly to China.

The People's Republic of China was founded in 1949. In 1951 the Roman Catholic Church was outlawed and the Communist state formed the Chinese Patriotic Catholic Alliance. Allegiance to the Holy Father was forbidden and the state appointed the "bishops."

Mao Zedong and the Communist state were responsible for the deaths of 55 million innocent Chinese. Since his death, his successors have made policies which have killed millions of innocents by abortions.

In reparation for these deaths and the 45th anniversary of the establishment of Chinese Communism we made our 1994 Year of the Family pilgrimage from Fatima to China, the anti-family country.

The Triumphant Queen of the World Peace Flight 101 was again organized by Dr. Rosalie Turton of the 101 Foundation. In 1982 Dr. Turton made a Peace Flight pilgrimage to China led by John Haffert. The pilgrims had intended to bring a Pilgrim Virgin statue of Our Lady of Fatima for China. On their way they had the Holy Father bless it in Rome and when he found out its intended purpose he kissed its feet!

The statue's entry to China was denied by the customs authorities and the statue was left behind in Hong Kong as the pilgrims entered China. This statue was born from the suffering of Communist hatred.

Bishop Cuthbert O'Gara was a Canadian who was ordained on the feast day of Our Lady of Fatima on May 13, 1938. He went to China as a missionary priest and was ordained as a Bishop. After the Communist Revolution he was arrested and paraded through the streets in his shorts while children threw rocks at him. He was placed in solitary confinement where he was tortured and scheduled for execution.

He began to pray 50 Rosaries a day and promised Our Lady that if he ever got out of China alive he would get a Pilgrim Virgin statue of Our Lady of Fatima for China. Three days before his scheduled execution he was released on a technicality.

He went to America and obtained a statue of Our Lady of Fatima carved by the original Fatima statue carver, José Thedim. Rosalie Turton said, "It is the most beautiful statue of Our Lady of Fatima, bar none!"

Bishop O'Gara obtained a promise from Father Philip Beebe and Father Owen Lally that if they ever went to China they would bring this statue with them. The Bishop died on the anniversary of Our Lady of Fatima and of his ordination, at noon on May 13, 1968.

Soon thereafter John Haffert wrote a magazine article entitled "Should a Pilgrim Virgin go to China?" Father Lally read the article and told Father Beebe, "We're the ones that have the statue and this is the one that should go to China." So they met with John Haffert on May 13, 1981 at 11 a.m. to tell him so. John was leaving for Fatima that day and told the priests that he didn't think a China pilgrimage was practical.

It was noon and at that moment the telephone rang. John listened and slowly replaced the receiver. He turned to the priests and said, "The Pope has just been shot! We're going to go to China with Our Lady of Fatima. I don't know how and I don't know when but we're going!" This decision was made under Divine Providence at the exact time and date of Our Lady of Fatima's apparition and Bishop O'Gara's death.

And so it was that one year later John Haffert, Rosalie Turton, Father Lally and Father Beebe and many pilgrims brought Bishop O'Gara's statue of Our Lady of Fatima to the gates of China only to be left in Hong Kong for her entry on another day - the day of the Triumphant Queen of the World Peace Flight Pilgrimage.

Our goal was to enter China with the International Pilgrim Virgin statue of Our Lady of Fatima.

PART TWO

The Pilgrimage to China

6. The Meaning of Pilgrimage

A pilgrimage is prayer in action. It is a living prayer, containing all of the dimensions of human activity - physical, spiritual and emotional. The pilgrimage begins with making the decision as to whether or not to go. The pros and the cons are weighed. All considerations are pondered. Should I go alone? Will my spouse join me? If my spouse doesn't join me, will my spouse resent my going? Can I afford it? Won't it be dangerous and tiring? Why travel so far when I can do so much good right where I am? Doesn't my spouse/family/children/job/parish/neighbor/etc. need me? On the other hand, is God calling me? Are the circumstances being peacefully arranged? Am I free of worry and anxiety and at peace about going? Yes!

Then Satan starts. "Nothing will change," he murmurs. "You will come back as empty as you are now. Nobody needs you. You could lose your job or alienate your spouse." But if the still, small voice appeals to your heart and says, "Come, do not be afraid for I go before you always," we discern His will, respond to His call and come after Him.

Pilgrim Jackie Galley discerned His will to come. She had suppressed any thought of going on the pilgrimage as it seemed impossible. However, shortly before Our Lady's birthday on September 8, her thoughts began to focus on going. On September 8 she attended an apparition of Our Lady to pilgrim visionary Gianna Sullivan and she asked Our Lady that if she was indeed calling her to go to the Holy Land, would she please give her a "tangible sign"? Later a lady came up to her and said, "I just wanted to give you this Rosary from the Holy Land!" She got her "tangible sign" and said "Yes" to Our Lady's call.

Pilgrim Edna Corrigan didn't think that she'd be able to go on the pilgrimage for which she had already paid her deposit. The pain from her rheumatoid arthritis was getting increasingly worse. Then one night she woke up in great pain but suddenly felt warmth come over her entire body from head to toe. After a few minutes it left and so did all of her pain! She said "Yes" to Our Lady's call.

Pilgrim Tina Steo, wife of our video photographer, was not raised with devotion to Our Lady and was a newcomer to pilgrimages. She wrote a poem called "A Prayer to Mother" and said,

> I love the Lord, Jesus your Son
> With a full and child-like heart,
> But you, gentle woman, I know not
> This pilgrimage is my start.
>
> Five years ago, I sought your Son
> He brought me to His hands,
> And now I find another pair
> Leading me across all lands.
>
> Here's my hand to place in yours
> My trust in you devout,
> Cloak me in your love and peace
> And lead me from all doubt.
>
> And so,
>
> Hail Mary, full of grace
> The Lord is with you,
> Protect this journey of peace
> And bring all to renew.

Essentially a pilgrimage is a renewal by picking up our cross and following in the footsteps of Jesus who said, "Whoever wishes to be my follower must deny his very self, take up his cross each day, and follow in my steps." Lk 9:23.

And so the pilgrims took up their crosses, formed Our Lady's Army and, in answer to the call of Jesus, they came. Some had to sell a piece of land or deplete meager savings. Many left behind spouses and families who sacrificially supported the pilgrimage. For those who responded to Our Lady's call, seemingly insurmountable obstacles disappeared.

Jesus told Dorothy Romano, "Much will be accomplished on this trip and I want all to know how much I love them. My children delight Me and I delight in their prayers. I have called you on a mission of great importance. It is imperative that you remain in a spirit of prayer and contemplation."

7. Our Lady's Army

Our Lady's Army of 425 blue-jacketed pilgrims, including sixteen priests, arrived at Kennedy airport in New York City on the afternoon of October 12, 1994. We had plenty of waiting time to renew old acquaintances and make new ones.

The pilgrims were of all ages and came from all over America, Ireland, the Philippines and Trinidad. We even had a young mother, Karen, and her three small children, all of whom were soon "adopted" by other pilgrims. The common denominator of all of the pilgrims was their simple, child-like faith that Mary, Our Mother, was in charge and that all would be well.

Our Lady told Dorothy Romano,

> You have been selected from among many, not because you are great, but because you are small. Hold my hand tightly and do not let go. Perilous days await you, but this mission will not be disrupted if you heed my requests.
>
> I tell you that you are my Army. Look to your shepherds for advice and counsel. Pay attention to what they say; my Son is speaking through them. In all things, dear children, choose to love those around you and do not be remiss in your prayers.

The maneuvers and bivouacs of Our Lady's Army presented many opportunities for sacrifice, as everyone's patience and kindness was tested to the limits. We waited long hours at airport terminals, sat on waiting planes and buses, ate poor food and had little sleep. We attended daily Mass, prayed up to eight daily Rosaries and the Divine Mercy Chaplet, attended holy hours and all-night vigils of Eucharistic Adoration and fasted on Fridays on bread and water. These were all offered to Jesus through Mary for the success of our mission.

We left on our chartered Boeing 747 airplane on October 12 and began our pattern of a constant state of prayer with the recitation of the Exorcism Prayer of St. Michael to defend us in our spiritual battle.

As I passed out lapel pins of Our Lady of Guadalupe on the airplane, many pilgrims smelled an overwhelming aroma of roses. Our Lady had given us the sign of her presence.

We had with us the International Pilgrim Virgin Statue of Our Lady of Fatima, the Missionary Image of Our Lady of Guadalupe and the Traveling Image of Jesus King of All Nations.

The statue and images in procession.

Our Lady's Army 35

Some of Our Lady's Army and their priests.

8. The Statue and Images

The International Pilgrim Virgin Statue of Our Lady of Fatima, the Missionary Image of Our Lady of Guadalupe and the Traveling Image of Jesus King of All Nations were the same ones that had accompanied many of these same pilgrims to the crownings in Red Square in Russia two years before.

The Pilgrim Virgin statue left Fatima for the first time in 1947. Many wonders accompanied the statue on its Journey. Doves flew down on the statue and remained at its base despite the pressing crowd and noise just as the dove alighted on the image of Jesus King of All Nations 45 years later. Also the statue shed tears just as the Missionary Image did 45 years later. Many cures and conversions followed the statue.

Pope Pius XII referred to the statue and said, "It is the Queen of Angels herself who goes forth ... from this sanctuary of Fatima where heaven permitted us to crown her Queen of the World ... to make jubilee visits to all her dominions. At her passing through America as through Europe," the Pope said, "marvels of grace are multiplied in such a way that we can hardly believe what we see taking place."

The Missionary Image of Our Lady of Guadalupe is an exact photographic replica of the original Miraculous Image which Our Lady left on Blessed Juan Diego's cloak in 1531. In 1991, it was blessed and commissioned by the Abbot of the Basilica of Our Lady of Guadalupe and by the late Cardinal Juan Jesus Posados to journey on a mission to end abortion and convert millions to the Sacred Heart of Jesus through the Immaculate Heart of Mary.

Since then it has journeyed on this mission throughout America and the world bringing many signs and wonders. The sun is frequently seen as a colorful, spinning wonder or as a large globe in the sky surrounded by a blue halo cloud and a round rainbow. The image has cried tears of oil and rose petals have miraculously flaked from it.

Our Lady of Guadalupe is pregnant in her image as is told in chapter 12 of the Book of Revelation, "A great sign appeared in the sky, a woman clothed with the sun, with the moon under her feet ... pregnant with child." Rev 12:1-2. Her pregnancy is also shown by the sign of the Aztec sash that she wears and by medical doctors who say that she exhibits the signs of a pregnant woman.

One of the continuing wonders of the image is that Our Lady manifests the heartbeat of the unborn Christ child in her womb. Many have felt this fetal heartbeat and nurses have even heard it with a stethoscope! This is Our Lady's message that the unborn is a child and not a choice.

There also have been many conversions, healings and reconciliations. Many mothers who contemplated abortions have chosen life for their unborn children. At least twenty abortion killing centers have closed shortly after prayerful Visitations by the Image. Two of these closings were announced on the Feast Day of Our Lady of Guadalupe!

Our Lady of Guadalupe said in modern revelations that "in my plan the Journey of my Image throughout all of the Americas is necessary ... I want you to immediately place your entire pro-life force and efforts under my banner as your Lady of Guadalupe ... Together, my dear children, we will end the horrible evil of abortion. I want millions to see my Image, the Woman Clothed With the Sun. I will melt their hearts to conversion."

Pope John Paul prophesied with reference to the original Miraculous Image of Our Lady of Guadalupe that "the light of the Gospel of Christ will shine out over the whole world by means of the Miraculous Image of His Mother."

The Image of Jesus King of All Nations was revealed to two American mystics. Jesus expressed His desire to reign in mercy in all hearts so that His reign will be recognized on earth and there will be unity with one flock and one shepherd. He also requested the proclamation of the dogma of Mary as Mediatrix of All Graces.

Bishop Enrique Hernandez Rivera of Caguas, Puerto Rico, where some of the revelations occurred said that he "recognized the need to foster more devotion to Our Lord and Savior Jesus the Christ, True King of All Nations." He wished the promoters of the Devotion "all the best in your efforts of spreading the message of Christ to all who invoke Him by this title."

Father Albert Herbert referred to the Devotion as "one of the last great efforts of Our Lord to pour out His mercy before His justice descends upon mankind in the Great Chastisements."

The Image of Jesus King of All Nations shows Him crowned and holding a scepter of mercy in His right hand. Above the scepter are three concentric rings which appear like an atom which symbolizes unity in God, in His Church, in nations and in Him. The small particle in the atom symbolizes the Church and Our Lady, both espoused to God. Rays of light shine from His wounds which symbolize His merciful graces. Blood flows from his wounded Sacred Heart upon all nations which symbolizes His love.

Jesus said, "This Image is a sign that I rule heaven and earth, and My Kingdom, My Reign, is near at hand. Give this Image to mankind as a source of graces and of peace. My Most Holy Mother is preparing the great triumph. The triumph of her Immaculate Heart ushers in the Reign of My Love and Mercy. Tremendous will be the miracles of grace that I will work through this Image and Devotion of Mine. This Image, My child, must become known."

To help make this Image known, the Traveling Image of Jesus King of All Nations was painted and brought on Visitations around the world. After a Visitation to the Philippines in 1992, Jesus said, "I am very pleased with My Image traveling. I promise, My child, that as long as this Image of Mine travels, so will I have Mercy on this world. Let souls of All Nations come before Me in My Image!"

The Image has journeyed throughout the world and has been displayed before millions of people. Many signs, wonders, healings and conversions have been reported.

A daughter prayed the devotional prayers for her elderly sick mother. She saw a vision of nine special angels which Jesus promises to the beneficiary of these prayers. Similarly, another daughter prayed the devotional prayers for her mother who was in a hopeless coma. Jesus promises many spiritual, physical, emotional and psychological healings for those who pray these prayers. Her mother recovered from the coma.

Armed with the statue, the Images, Rosaries, prayers and the sacraments, Our Lady's Army began their pilgrimage to China through Fatima, the Holy Land and the Philippines to conclude in thanksgiving at Akita, Japan. Signs and wonders, danger and grace awaited us.

The International Pilgrim Virgin Statue of Our Lady of Fatima

9. Fatima, Portugal

Our first place of pilgrimage was to Fatima, Portugal to celebrate the 77th anniversary of Our Lady's last apparition there on October 13, 1917. On our way to Fatima we stopped at the Village of Santarem.

Here in the thirteenth century a wife sought advice from a witch in order to obtain her husband's favor. The witch advised her to steal a consecrated host. She did so but, to her horror, the host began to bleed. So she placed it in a trunk so that no one would see it. However, light began to shine out from the trunk in the middle of the night. She called the pastor and he reverently led a procession of the host back to the Church where it has since remained incorrupt as a lasting sign of the real presence of Jesus in the Eucharistic host.

We arrived at the Fatima Plaza with the Missionary Image and the Image of Jesus King of All Nations too late to join the entrance procession with the original Fatima statue which had just begun. The Plaza was filled with approximately 500,000 people so we just placed the images down in the middle of the crowd. At that point, some guards approached us and told us that we had to move the images to the extreme rear of the Plaza. Rather than argue, we obeyed and our obedience was rewarded.

As the Fatima statue was processed from the center of the Plaza towards the altar, we processed the Images from the center towards the rear, so most of the faithful had the opportunity of venerating both the statue and the Images. We ended our procession to the rear just as the procession to the altar ended and the Mass began with providential good timing.

Our Lady appeared to Irish visionary, Beaulah Lynch, after she received Communion. On behalf of all of the pilgrims, Our Lady said, "Peace, I have called you and you have come." And then Beaulah saw us all as little children running towards Our Lady and being surrounded and gathered up in her mantle.

The Image of Jesus King of All Nations and the Missionary Image of Our Lady of Guadalupe overlooking a half million faithful in Fatima Plaza with statues of the holy Family and Divine Mercy.

10. Holy Land, Israel

Jesus told Dorothy Romano, "I have planned this time together in the land of my birth and I want you to savor it. Together we will climb the hills and walk the paths of My homeland. I want you to see the place of My birth and touch and feel the place where I died. I did all of this for you and you were always in My Heart."

All of the following Holy Land sites were visited by the pilgrims although not in the order set forth. The sites are arranged in the chronological order of the life of Christ so that in our imagination we can walk in His footsteps and have a better appreciation of the sites. At each of the sites pertinent scriptures were read for our meditation on the significance of the site and the actions of Jesus.

Bethlehem. Bethlehem means house of bread and it was prophesied, "You, Bethlehem, land of Judah, are by no means least among the rulers of Judah; since from you shall come a ruler, who is to shepherd my people Israel." Mt 2:6.

Bethlehem lies five miles south of Jerusalem on a hill about 2,500 feet above sea level. "So Joseph set out from the town of Nazareth in Galilee and travelled up to Judea, to the town of David called Bethlehem, since he was of David's house and line, in order to be registered together with Mary his betrothed who was with child. While they were there, the time came for her to have her child, and she gave birth to a son, her first born. She wrapped him in swaddling clothes, and laid him in a manger because there was no room for them at the inn." Lk 2:1-20.

Some of the pilgrims arrived at their hotel in Bethlehem only to find that for them too, there was no room for them at the inn. Unfortunately there were no reservations for them. One pilgrim exclaimed with dismay, "There is no room for us in the inn!" They were then taken to the cellar of a convent with rooms without water located 150 feet from the cave of the Nativity. They joyfully shared some of the privations of the Holy Family.

In Bethlehem at the Church of the Nativity we celebrated an early Christmas Mass and sang Christmas hymns. An entrance led from the Church to a rectangular shaped cave, 35 feet by 10 feet in size. It is lit by 48 lamps and a silver star marks the spot where Jesus was born. It is inscribed in Latin, "Hic de Maria Virgine Jesus Christus Natus est". (Here Jesus Christ was born of the Virgin Mary.) "Glory to God in the highest and on earth peace to men of good will." Lk 2:14.

Here we also visited the cave of the burial of the Holy Innocents and asked them to intercede for their innocent unborn brothers and sisters killed today by abortion. "Then was fulfilled what had been said through Jeremiah the prophet: 'A voice was heard in Ramah, sobbing and loud lamentation; Rachel weeping for her children, and she would not be consoled, since they were no more.'" Mt 2:17-18.

We also lamented our armed service people who were no more as we celebrated the 50th anniversary of the day that pilgrim George Ritchie was shot down while on a bombing mission over Cologne, Germany. He spent time in various Nazi prison camps and escaped three times. We thanked God that he wasn't recaptured after his third escape! He walked for 36 days at night on his return to Allied lines. His Armenian friend who looked Jewish didn't fare as well. He was taken down an alley and shot to death.

The Star marks the place of Christ's birth in the grotto beneath the central altar in the Church of the Nativity in Bethlehem.

Nazareth. This city was the place chosen by God for the Annunciation of the virgin birth of His Son. It was His home until manhood. Lk 1:26-35. Here "the Word became flesh and dwelt among us." Jn 1:14. Joseph "went and dwelt in a town called Nazareth, so that what had been spoken through the prophets might be fulfilled, 'He shall be called a Nazorean.'" Mt 2:23.

One of the tour busses got stranded here because of a flat tire. However, the pilgrims had the right attitude and laughed at their predicament saying that it was a good place to get stranded as Jesus Himself had been stranded here for thirty years!

Here at the Church of the Annunciation we celebrated Mass and sung Schubert's "Ave Maria" in memory of the angel Gabriel's Annunciation to Mary, "Hail Mary, full of grace, the Lord is with you!" Lk 1:28. Inscribed beneath the altar of the Grotto of the Annunciation are the words, "Here the Word was made flesh."

Just as the priest set down the chalice after the consecration, a tremendous thunderclap was heard and torrential rains fell on the roof in this usually arid place.

Unfortunately, Nazareth, His own hometown, was the first place to reject Jesus. As He said, "No prophet is accepted in his own native place." Lk 4:24. The first attempt on Jesus' life was also made at Nazareth as "they rose up, drove Him out of the town, and led Him to the brow of the hill on which their town had been built, to hurl Him down headlong. But He passed through the midst of them and went away." Lk 4:29.

The Church of the Annunciation.

The River Jordan. After Jesus left Nazareth, He went to the River Jordan where John the Baptist was preaching and baptizing. He went there to be baptized by John. Mt 3:13. "After Jesus was baptized, He came up from the water and behold, the heavens were opened for Him and He saw the Spirit of God descending like a dove and coming upon Him. And a voice came from the heavens, saying, 'This is my beloved Son, with whom I am well pleased.'" Mt 3:16-17.

We too went to this strange river which flows from the snow-covered heights of Mount Hermon to the depths of the Dead Sea along a winding bed 160 miles as it meanders, but only 65 miles in a straight line. We waded into the river, blessed ourselves with the water and renewed our own Baptismal promises by renouncing Satan, his pomps and works and totally consecrating ourselves to Jesus through Mary according to the formula of St. Louis de Montfort in imitation of the spirituality of the Holy Father.

Pilgrims renew their Baptismal promises in the River Jordan.

Jericho. The city of Jericho is located in the Jordan Valley about 25 miles east of Jerusalem. It looks like a green valley in the middle of the sun-baked desert.

The traditional spot where Jesus was baptized in the River Jordan is near the city of Jericho near where Joshua crossed the river to take the Promised Land. See Joshua 3:13-17. Jesus is the new Joshua leading us into the eternal Promised Land of heaven.

Here we sang the rousing Gospel hymn, "Joshua fit the Battle of Jericho" and commemorated his victory over the city in the 13th century B.C. Jericho was settled about nine thousand years ago and is the oldest city in the world. It was fortified with walls fifteen feet high and nine feet wide which tumbled at the blast of the Israelites' trumpets. See Joshua 6.

Its location was of great strategic value since it commanded a ford across the Jordan River and it had a good source of water from the spring that was sweetened by the salt of the prophet Elisha. See 2 Kings 2:19. This spring is the source of Jericho's green oasis. From Jericho the Jordan River empties into the Dead Sea to the south.

The map of Israel shows the Jordan River running through the heart-shaped Sea of Galilee in the north which receives it and gives it to the south where it empties into the Dead Sea which is 1,300 feet below sea level, the lowest spot on the earth and dead to all life because of its salt content.

The Sea of Galilee is analogous to a spiritually living heart which receives and gives life while the Dead Sea is analogous to a heart which only takes life and is spiritually dead.

About five miles west of Jericho is the Mount of the Temptation to which Jesus retired immediately after His baptism in the Jordan River. It is a totally desolate mountain about 2000 feet high and covered with rocks, rubble, and desert sand. "Filled with the Holy Spirit, Jesus returned from the Jordan and was led by the Spirit into the desert for forty days, to be tempted by the devil." Lk 4:1-2.

Blessed peace from the oldest city, Jericho.

Cana. Jesus worked His first miracle at a wedding feast in the town of Cana where He turned water into wine. Here the married pilgrims recalled their own Canas and renewed their marriage vows.

Pilgrim Ed Norse wrote the poem, "The Wine",

> Who is this man, who takes these jars,
> And tells the servants what to do?
> Who is this woman crowned with stars,
> Whose Son would start the world anew?
>
> The sign at Cana, that we see,
> Is one with meaning deep and vast.
> Its purpose there for you and me,
> To understand what truly lasts.
>
> For water into wine must turn,
> To satisfy the wedding guests.
> But in this tale, so must we learn
> That sacrifice to God is test.
>
> If we would drink the blood of Christ
> We need God's grace, we need God's light.

We meditated on Our Lady's words to the waiters, "Do whatever He tells you." Jn 2:5. After she said this, she and Jesus "went down to Capernaum ... " Jn 2:12.

Cana Church mural showing Jesus blessing the jars of water.

Capernaum. Capernaum is located on the northwest shore of the Sea of Galilee, 2 1/2 miles south from where the River Jordan enters it. It was a busy city located on the trade route to Damascus during the time of Jesus. He made His second home here in St. Peter's hometown and it became the center of His mission for the next 20 months.

Here Jesus preached to the people and manifested His goodness, mercy, compassion and omnipotence by His many miracles and mighty deeds. Unfortunately, they had little influence on the conversion of the people and Jesus prophesied against the city.

"And as for you, Capernaum: 'Will you be exalted to heaven? You will go down to the nether-world.' For if the mighty deeds done in your midst had been done in Sodom, it would have remained until this day. But I tell you, it will be more tolerable for the land of Sodom on the day of judgment than for you." Mt 12:23-24.

Jesus' prophecy about the ungrateful city was fulfilled and today Capernaum is no more than a heap of rubble near the lakeshore. The ruins of the synagogue remain where Jesus taught, cured the demoniac (see Mk 1:21-26) and raised Jarius' daughter from the dead (see Mt 9:18-26). About 50 yards to the south are the remains of St. Peter's home where Jesus cured his mother-in-law (see Mt 8:14-17) and the paralytic man when he was let down through the roof (see Mt 9:1-8).

Here we celebrated Mass in a Church built over the excavated house of St. Peter. The Church has a glass floor in the center and is elevated by eight pedestals above the excavation so that you can look down into the room and hearth which was the center of the house, as did the men who let down the paralytic through the roof. The Church overlooks the beautiful Sea of Galilee.

Pilgrim Ed Norse wrote the poem " Capernaum",
> Beneath this floor is where you dwelt
> With Peter and his mother-in-law.
> Throughout your ministry you dealt
> With all you heard and all you saw.
>
> Your life in Nazareth would end,
> You came here to begin anew.
> The message that to man you send
> Would bring them back to God renewed.

So here, by Sea of Galilee
You chose disciples as your own.
The future that we now can see,
Had left unturned not single stone.

You came to pick, to love, to teach
Help mind grasp all that you did preach!

The Sea of Galilee. The Sea of Galilee is 13 miles long, 7 miles wide and 32 miles in circumference. It is abundant in fish which are still caught in nets as in biblical times. We ate a meal of St. Peter's fish (tilapias) at the beautiful seaport of Tiberias which was built by Herod Antipas in 26 A.D. The site was described by the Jewish historian Josephus as "the ambition of nature."

From Tiberias we embarked on a Peace Boat cruise on the Sea of Galilee. The azure blue water and cooling breeze helped us to contemplate the command of Jesus that stilled the violent storm (see Mt 8:23-27) and His walk on the stormy water (see Mt 14:22-23). It was near these shores that Jesus called many of His apostles (see Mt 4:18-20) and spoke to the multitudes from Peter's boat (see Mk 3:7-12).

Peace Boat pilgrims on the Sea of Galilee.

Jerusalem. Standing proudly amidst the arid Judean hills is the city of Jerusalem, queen of the world's cities for over 30 centuries. This was God's choice for the center of monotheism and is the religious capital of half of the human race - the Jews who follow Moses, the Christians who follow Jesus and the Moslems who follow Mohammed.

This city where peace is always preached has also been a city of wars. More wars have been fought at its gates than in any other city of the world. It has been besieged more than 50 times, conquered 36 times and destroyed 10 times.

Jesus travelled about 110 miles by foot to Jerusalem at least three times a year with the Holy Family from the time of His youth for the Feasts of Passover, Pentecost and Tabernacles. He travelled from Nazareth southeast to the Jordan Valley, south down the Jordan Valley to Jericho and from there west through the desert up to Jerusalem. From Jericho to Jerusalem the land rises in the course of 25 miles from about 1000 feet below sea level to 2,500 feet above sea level, through a waterless desert with a change in elevation of almost 4000 feet! To say that Jesus went "up" to Jerusalem is literally true.

"They were on the way, going up to Jerusalem, and Jesus went ahead of them. They were amazed, and those who followed were afraid. Taking the Twelve aside again, he began to tell them what was going to happen to Him. 'Behold, we are going up to Jerusalem, and the Son of Man will be handed over to the chief priests and the scribes, and they will condemn Him to death and hand Him over to the Gentiles, who will mock Him, spit upon Him, scourge Him, and put Him to death, but after three days He will rise.'" Mk 10:32-34.

"After He had said this, He proceeded on His journey up to Jerusalem. As He drew near to Bethpage and Bethany at the place called the Mount of Olives, ... they brought (a colt) to Jesus, threw their cloaks over the colt, and helped Jesus to mount. As He rode along, the people were spreading their cloaks on the road; and now as He was approaching the slope of the Mount of Olives, the whole multitude of His disciples began to praise God aloud with joy for all the mighty deeds they had seen. They proclaimed: 'Blessed is the king who comes in the name of the Lord. Peace in heaven and glory in the highest.'" Lk 19:28-38.

In imitation of Jesus, pilgrim Father Walter Winrich mounted a providentially provided white colt and rode it down the slope of the Mount of Olives as we processed along carrying olive branches, skipping and singing "The King of Glory Comes" and "Blessed Is He Who Comes in the Name of the Lord."

As Jesus drew near the city of Jerusalem, "He saw the city and wept over it, saying, 'If this day you only knew what makes for peace - but now it is hidden from your eyes. For the days are coming upon you when your enemies will raise a palisade against you; they will encircle you and hem you in on all sides. They will smash you to the ground and your children within you, and they will not leave one stone upon another within you because you did not recognize the time of your visitation." Lk 19:41-44.

This prophecy was literally fulfilled by the Roman General Titus and his army in the year 70 A.D. when they besieged Jerusalem and utterly destroyed the city leaving "not one stone upon another" except for the Western Wall of the Temple.

This wall still stands with its huge blocks as the holiest shrine of the Jewish world. It was left standing by Titus as a reminder of the might of the Roman army which had the strength to destroy the rest of the Temple and the city.

The Cenacle in Jerusalem is the room of the Last Supper where Jesus instituted the Eucharist and the priesthood (Lk 22:19-20); where He appeared after His Resurrection (Jn 20:19-29) and where the Holy Spirit descended at Pentecost (Acts 2:1-4). We followed Jesus from here in our imagination as He left His Last Supper to His Agony in the Garden. "Then He went, as was His custom, to the Mount of Olives, and the disciples followed Him." Lk 22:39.

The Garden of Gethsemane is located east of Jerusalem across the Kidron Valley at the base of the Mount of Olives. It appears today as it did during the time of Christ even with olive trees that date back to that time period!

The beautiful Church of Gethsemane is located here. Just before the altar a large part of the top of the rock over which Jesus prayed is exposed. This Church is also called the Church of All Nations because sixteen nations contributed to its construction.

Here the Image of Jesus King of All Nations was particularly welcomed because of the significance of the name of the Church.

After we celebrated Mass here, Our Lady appeared over the altar to the Irish visionary Mary Casey. Mary was very happy to see Our Lady for the first time in over 7 years. Our Lady said, "Peace, I will lead you and I promise my special protection over you. Happy are you who work for peace, you love me. Make more people love me. Pray with us and make everything you do be a prayer. Be aware of my Son's presence. I am always with you. I will never abandon you. Go in peace."

We tried to be more aware of her Son's presence and meditated on His plea made during His Agony in the Garden, "Could you not keep watch with me for one hour?" Mt 26:40. Father Neil preached that the way to answer Jesus' plea is through Eucharistic adoration by which we acknowledge the real presence of His body and blood, soul and divinity.

"Then the whole assembly of them arose and brought Him before Pilate." Lk 23:1. "Then Pilate took Jesus and had Him scourged. And the soldiers wove a crown out of thorns and placed it on His head . . . ." Jn 19:1-2. "Then he handed Him over to them to be crucified." Jn 19:16.

These events took place in the Antonia Fortress which was razed to the ground with the rest of Jerusalem by the Roman General Titus in 70 A.D. Today the Convent of the Sisters of Zion locates the scene of these events. Here begins Jesus "Via Dolorosa" (Way of Sorrows) which is the traditional Way of the Cross from the place of judgment to His crucifixion on Calvary.

There are 14 stations on the Via Dolorosa of which 9 are scriptural and 5 traditional. The first two stations are located at the Convent, 7 are located in the streets and the last 5 are located within the Church of the Holy Sepulchre. "So they took Jesus, and carrying the cross Himself He went out to what is called the Place of the Skull, in Hebrew, Golgotha." Jn 19:16-17.

We joined Him in spirit carrying replica crosses throughout the streets along the Via Dolorosa commemorating Jesus' Stations of the Cross to the Church of the Holy Sepulchre. This Church is the most sacred place of Christianity since it marks the place of Christ's Crucifixion as well as His Resurrection. Part of the floor rests on the actual rock of Calvary which can be seen under an altar dedicated to Our Lady of Sorrows.

"Now in the place where He had been crucified there was a garden, and in the garden a new tomb, in which no one had yet been buried. So they laid Jesus there because of the Jewish preparation day; for the tomb was close by." Jn 19:41-42. Jesus' tomb was located at the foot of Calvary.

The present monument in the Church of the Holy Sepulchre has a marble slab which marks the place where Jesus' body was laid. It is believed that the original stone is located beneath the one that is displayed. This also marks the spot of His Resurrection at which the angels asked the holy women, "Why do you seek the living one among the dead? He is not here, but He has been raised." Lk 24:5-6. Alleluia!

We landed in the Holy Land on the day of an attempted rescue by the Israeli Army of one of their soldiers who was held hostage by The Islamic Resistance Movement (Hamas) which demanded the release of 200 Moslem prisoners. The Israelis refused, and in the rescue attempt the Moslems killed the hostage, two of them were killed and 12 Israeli soldiers were wounded.

On the same day, two members of Hamas opened fire in a shopping center in Jerusalem and killed 3 people and wounded 14. Our Holy Land pilgrimage began with terrorism. One of the pilgrims was wearing a pin of Our Lady of Guadalupe. Soon it began weeping tears of oil.

However, after several days of prayer and fasting by the peace pilgrims, peace was unexpectedly announced between Israel and Jordan. This put an end to their formal 46-year state of war. "Peace be upon you, God's peace," said Jordanian King Hussein. "All the children of Abraham will remember this dawning of a new era of peace."

Israeli Prime Minister Yitzhak Rabin responded that the two nations would "draw on the springs of our great spiritual resources, to forgive the anguish we caused each other, to clear the minefields that divided us for so many years."

Also during our stay in the Holy Land, the Combined Loyalist Military Command, the pro-British Protestant extremists in Northern Ireland announced a cease-fire following the Irish Republican Army's announcement the month before. Amazingly their statement expressed "abject and true remorse" for all innocent victims of the Troubles.

This was followed by a new accord which was reached between the United States and North Korea by which its nuclear facilities will be opened to international inspection and it will rejoin the nuclear non-proliferation treaty. "I hope the improving of bilateral relations will make a significant contribution to peace in Asia and the rest of the world," said Kang So Ju, North Korean Vice Foreign Minister. Peace was flowing like a river! ... and we joyfully sang the song.

Our Jewish tour guide attributed the Jordanian peace announcement to our prayers. She said, "Thank you from the biggest part of my heart for praying for peace for my country! I am so impressed that you left your homes and families to travel around the world for peace. I think it is great. I don't know all the words to describe how great it is. I feel privileged to have been with you and again thank you for being here with us and for us especially on this day."

She was referring to our last day in the Holy Land when a Moslem suicide-terrorist had the last word and exploded a bomb on a crowded bus in Tel Aviv killing 22 people just as we approached the city. As we brought peace, the voice of hatred protested.

The walled city of Jerusalem as seen from the Mount of Olives and the place where Jesus wept over the city.

56 The Pilgrimage to China

Pilgrims carrying a cross on the Via Dolorosa.

Father Walter Winrich imitating Jesus riding a colt down the Mount of Olives towards Jerusalem.

Calvary where Jesus was crucified, now located in the Church of the Holy Sepulchre.

11. Manila, Philippines

We were greeted in the airport at Manila in the Philippines by hundreds of clergy and faithful including a band!

The Philippines have a population of 74 million, of whom 85% are Catholic, located over 7101 islands. It is the land of one of Our Lady's greatest victories. The corrupt and powerful regime of President Ferdinand Marcos had ruled over the Philippines since 1965. In 1972 he imposed martial law and canceled the elections scheduled for 1973. The people patiently prayed for Our Lady to triumph.

Our Lady raised up Benigno "Ninoy" Aquino, Jr. He was imprisoned by the Marcos regime for almost eight years in solitary confinement during which he had a vision of Our Lady. He constantly prayed the Rosary.

In 1980 he left the Philippines in a self-imposed exile to the United States. On August 21, 1983 he returned to the Philippines to confront the corrupt regime and was slain by the government military "escort" on the tarmac as he left the airplane. He died with his Rosary clasped in his hand. His widow Corazon "Cory" Aquino was informed and said, "The children and I cried when I told them of the bad news. After a few minutes, we all knelt down to pray the Rosary and ask the Blessed Mother for help."

The Philippine Bishops, led by Cardinal Jaime Sin of Manila, consecrated the nation to the Immaculate Heart of Mary on

December 8, 1983. In 1984 the weeping Pilgrim Virgin statue visited Manila where two million Filipinos gathered to pay her homage and Cory Aquino presented one of Ninoy's shirts during the offertory to symbolize her offering of the life of her husband.

In 1985 the Philippine Bishops declared a Marian Year and five million Filipinos consecrated themselves to the Immaculate Heart of Mary and joined a Rosary pledge for freedom, justice and peace. Cardinal Sin announced that a miracle would take place at the end of the Marian Year.

This miracle took place in Manila between February 22-25, 1986. It came as a dramatic sequel to an electoral contest between President Marcos and Cory Aquino. On February 13 the Catholic Bishops' Conference condemned the elections as fraudulent. On February 15 Marcos was proclaimed the winner but the Filipino people refused to accept this.

On February 22 Defense Minister Juan Ponce Enrile and General (now President) Fidel Ramos called for Marcos to resign and barricaded themselves with about 300 soldiers at Camp Aguinaldo. Cardinal Sin asked all cloistered nuns to prostrate themselves before the Blessed Sacrament. He asked the people to take to the streets and to support the soldiers. This began the People Power Revolution.

Millions of non-violent Filipinos took to the streets and prayed and fasted for three days. Marcos sent in the Marines to capture the rebellious soldiers but a human barricade stopped them one mile from the Camp. Nuns held off soldiers while on their knees praying their Rosaries. People holding up statues of Our Lady of Fatima held off tanks. Our Lady even appeared to the startled soldiers in the sky and said, "Don't shoot my children!"

This scene is memorialized at a chapel of perpetual adoration located in the middle of the Edsa, Manila's main street. A mural of the events, including Our Lady's apparition, encircles the chapel wall. This People Power Marian Revolution served as the model for those soon to follow in Poland and the Soviet Union.

On the third day, February 25, Marcos fled the country and Cory Aquino was installed as President of the Philippines. It was the Feast of Our Lady of Victory! This fulfilled the prophesied miracle of Cardinal Sin.

Our Lady and People Power hold off Marcos' tanks.

Mural at Manila's Edsa Memorial Chapel showing Our Lady's apparition stopping tanks and blessing People Power.

In 1992 the Missionary Image of Our Lady of Guadalupe and the Image of Jesus King of All Nations were welcomed to the Philippines. On December 12, the Feast Day of Our Lady of Guadalupe, two million faithful attended a Mass con-celebrated by Cardinals Sin and Mahoney with twelve bishops and sixty priests.

Cardinal Mahoney crowned the Missionary Image as the Patroness of the Philippine Islands, as she had been proclaimed by Pope Pius XI. The Mass concluded with the candlelit singing of "The Light of Christ" as a symbol and hope for reverence for life, peace and unity in the Philippines.

At Manila's World Youth Day in 1995, the Holy Father prayed before the Missionary Image which was placed in a truck converted to his private chapel before celebrating an outdoor Mass. In 1919 Pope Benedict XV proclaimed, "The Virgin of Guadalupe is the Protectress of the Pontiff." In 1979 Pope John Paul II invoked on his pontificate "the motherly protection and assistance of Our Lady of Guadalupe." She must have heard his prayers because the authorities uncovered a plot to assassinate him in the Philippines!

The Philippines were celebrating 400 years of the organized and hierarchical presence of the Church. The Holy Father said, "That first evangelization produced enduring fruits of Christian life and holiness, of civilizing action, of the transmission - especially through a strong family life - of fundamental human and civic values. ... The Church in the Philippines knows that it has a special vocation to bear witness to the Gospel in the heart of Asia."

Cardinal Roger Mahoney crowning Missionary Image of Our Lady of Guadalupe before Cardinal Jaime Sin and two million Filipino faithful.

Cardinal Jaime Sin blessing image of Jesus King of All Nations.

Pope John Paul II approaching his "truck chapel" where the Missionary Image of Our Lady of Guadalupe awaits him at Manila's 1995 World Youth Day.

We journeyed to the Philippines to prepare to bear witness to the Gospel in the heart of Asia and to promote strong family life in the Year of the Family by our attendance as delegates to The International Holy Family Year Congress.

As we approached the Philippines, Beaulah Lynch received a message from Our Lady that our priests were to go before the Blessed Sacrament in adoration with the laity. Our Lady said, "There will be little sleep and little rest from now on. This is a dangerous mission."

On the day of our arrival, Moslems kidnapped 21 Christians and held them as hostages. On the next day we encountered Typhoon Katring which killed 20 and left 85,000 homeless. We were off to a shaky start.

The typhoon brought 20 inches of heavy rains and strong winds. The wind knocked out windows in our hotel chapel and the candles that were burning inside. Our hotel went a day without electricity. Nevertheless, we bussed to Taal Cathedral, the largest in the Philippines. As we ran from the busses to the Cathedral, umbrellas were turned inside out, rain parkas blew straight out in the wind and the rains poured into the open Cathedral doors. This Cathedral had been used since the seventeenth century as a refuge in times of storms. We took full advantage of this use.

The next day we learned that the typhoon winds reached 100 miles per hour and one of the pilgrims retraced our route of the day before and witnessed vast devastation. Yet we were not hurt in any way.

Providentially, we celebrated with the Filipinos the 50th anniversary of the famous return of General Douglas McArthur to the Philippines during World War II. He once said that the Philippines "fastened me with a grip that never relaxed."

In 1942 he left the Philippines before the advancing Japanese troops and went to Australia promising to return. He kept his promise and waded ashore at Leyte in 1944 with the words, "I have returned. Rally to me! The guidance of divine God points the way. Follow in His name to the Holy Grail of righteous victory."

We were a new army of peace carrying our spiritual weapons of prayer and fasting for life and the family and following in His name to the Holy Grail of His righteous victory for the Holy Father's Year of the Family and his call for a culture of life and love.

At the Family Congress we attended Mass with eighteen Bishops and many priests from many countries concelebrating. We adopted resolutions that the Christian family should reverence life, stand against anti-life governmental action, pray the family Rosary, promote devotion to the Hearts of Jesus and Mary and to St. Joseph as a model of this devotion and practice the First Friday-First Saturday Communion of Reparation by attending Mass on those days, reciting the Rosary, receiving Confession and Communion and adoring the Blessed Sacrament with the intention of making reparation to the Hearts of Jesus and Mary for the sins of the world.

Dorothy Romano received a message from Jesus,

> My children delight Me and I want them to know that I am with them in a particular way during this stay in the Philippines.
>
> It is my will and intention that perpetual adoration be established and I desire that my people come before Me in vigils of reparation. If all would come before Me the tide could be turned, but they stay away. They flock to amusements, but they will not come to Me. My Eucharistic Heart beats with love, but I am spurned. You at least My people, console Me. Console Me and make intercession for those who will not. Come before the Blessed Sacrament and adore the God who made you.
>
> The purpose of this trip is to pray, to make intercession, to make atonement, and to ask for my Divine intervention. Pray and intercede for all of Asia. I want My heart to be established as a fountain of living water which will engulf all of Asia. I want to reside in the Philippines as King and it is My desire to reign in all hearts, not just some.

This was an echo of what Jesus revealed in the Jesus King of All Nations Devotion when He said, "I want to reign in all hearts! My throne on this earth remains in the hearts of all men. I most particularly reign in the Most Holy Eucharist, and in loving hearts that believe in Me, that speak with Me, and I tell you, My daughter that I do speak in the hearts of all men."

Our Lady told Dorothy Romano,

> Through the Mass My Son will conquer. Be aware of the great dignity of the Holy Sacrifice of the Mass. Dear children, I want you to unite your Rosaries mystically with the Holy Sacrifice being offered every day. Place your prayers in the chalice and be confident of my Son's ability to move heaven and earth. Nothing is impossible to God. No, nothing!
>
> I have come down from heaven to ask for your prayers. These visitations are coming to an end. I ask each and every one of you to be prepared for the days that lie ahead. Prepare yourselves through prayer and the sacraments. Convert and do penance. In this way you will stand firm. Rely on your mother who loves you and will defend you in the days of battle.

Filipino hospitality is legendary. People warmly greeted us at Masses and even gave up their seats with friendly smiles. They had beautiful processions and always honor Our Lady with flowers. Pedestrians always waved to our busses. Filipino jitneys proudly display Christian signs such as "Jesus Saves" and "Mama Mary Cares."

Mama Mary showed us that she really cares about *every* detail. Many of the pilgrims were getting sick so our doctors advised that we stock up on medicines before we went to China where we would be less likely to obtain them. So Ed Norse and I walked late at night through dark back alleys to a hospital pharmacy. We each picked out our medicines and then a lady pilgrim who was a nurse joined us and picked out hers. Neither she nor I had much Filipino money but Ed had some. To our dismay the pharmacist would not accept credit cards, would only take Filipino money and had no American money to make change.

Not to worry. Mama Mary was with us. The pharmacist totaled up our bills. Mine came to $40. Ed and the lady had enough Filipino money for me. Then Ed paid his bill using more Filipino money. But then, lo and behold, another lady pilgrim came in without Filipino money, rang up a bill for 975 pesos and said, "Well, Mary is just going to have to take care of this one!"

The rest of us dug down into our pockets and threw all of our pesos on the counter. It came to 976 pesos! One more peso than needed and everyone was ecstatic.

But we still had the matter of paying each other back in American money. The nurse had two $1 bills and the other lady paid off Ed with a $20 bill. But she owed the nurse $8 and paid her with a $10 bill and received the nurse's two $1 bills in change. The nurse then paid me the $10 she now had. Then I paid a $50 bill to Ed to pay him the $40 that I owed him. But Ed had no tens for change, only twenties. So he gave the nurse a $20 bill, she found two tens in change and Ed gave one to me in change for my $50 bill.

So everyone left with their medicines, exactly paid for in pesos, and with the exact change in American money! Our Lady was smiling upon this whole scene which was unbelievable and almost impossible to retell. Mama Mary cares!

We visited the Filipino visionary, Teresita of Lipa, who experienced a miraculous shower of 101 rose petals one month before the arrival of our Peace Flight 101. Similarly, the miraculous statue of Akita, Japan wept 101 times. The Philippines and Japan are the two countries which are the key to the conversion of China and, as the Holy Father said, the Philippines "has a special vocation to bear witness to the Gospel in the heart of Asia."

At Akita, Japan, the angel told Sister Agnes of the great significance of the number 101. The Eternal God represented by the "0" was surrounded by the first "1" which represented the First Eve who sinned and the second "1" which represented the Second Eve, Our Lady, who was sinless.

I doubted that exactly 101 rose petals had fallen, so I asked a Filipino friend of mine how Teresita knew that there were exactly 101 petals. She answered, "Because we counted each and every one of them!"

During the Second World War the Japanese rounded up 16,000 Filipino men, women and children and incarcerated them in the seminary at Lipa which was located about 50 miles south of Manila. There they bayoneted every one of them to death and set the seminary and bodies afire in a holocaust of innocents which definitely reached heaven. After the war a Carmelite convent was constructed on the spot and Our Lady came to her children.

The phenomena of the miraculous shower of 101 rose petals which occurred on the Feast of Our Lady of Sorrows, September 15, 1994, had their origin at the Lipa Carmel exactly 46 years earlier on September 15, 1948! Our Lady showered the rose petals in order to authenticate her messages given there. September 15, 1981 was also the 101st and last time that the Akita statue wept.

On September 15, 1948, the whole Lipa community came outside to attend the blessing by Bishop Obviar of a vine upon which Our Lady had appeared. During the ceremony Our Lady appeared to Teresita and asked her to kiss the ground and eat the grass, just as she had asked St. Bernadette at Lourdes a century before. Teresita thought, "Perhaps she is testing my obedience first of all and second, perhaps, she is also testing the humility that could accompany it because it is not a joke to eat the grass."

When she finished her humiliating act, she stood up and the entire community witnessed the first miraculous shower of rose petals! Like the roses from Juan Diego's tilma which was the sign for Bishop Zumarraga to believe, so too were the showered rose petals the sign for Bishop Obviar to believe.

Our Lady appeared for the last time at the vine on November 12, 1948. She said, "Spread the meaning of the Rosary because this will be the instrument for peace throughout the world. Tell the people that the Rosary must be said with devotion. Propagate the devotion to my Immaculate Heart. Do penance for priests and nuns but be not afraid, for the love of my Son will soften the hardest of hearts, and my motherly love will be their strength to crush the enemies of God.

"What I ask here is the same I asked at Fatima. I repeat to you that I am Mary, Mediatrix of All Grace." With this, she rose up to the clouds and disappeared.

The title "Mediatrix of All Grace" was next revealed at Amsterdam on November 15, 1951 when Our Lady appeared as Our Lady of All Nations and said,

> I come as Co-Redemptrix-Mediatrix at this time. Co-Redemptrix I was already at the Annunciation. This means that the Mother became Co-Redemptrix by the will of the Father.
>
> Tell your theologians this. Tell them moreover, that this will be the last dogma in Marian history. This picture shall prepare the way.

The picture of Our Lady of All Nations was the model for the Akita statue. Similarly, an image was revealed as part of the Jesus King of All Nations Devotion entitled, "Jesus Christ Mediator, Our Lady Mediatrix of All Graces." This image was drawn by the visionary whose hand was guided by Our Lady to represent her apparition. The image helps to explain the title of Our Lady Mediatrix of All Graces. As in the Amsterdam and Akita images, Our Lady stands on the world in front of the Cross as Co-Redemptrix and Mediatrix.

The Akita statue wept 101 times, the last time on September 15, 1981, Feast of Our Lady of Sorrows. 101 rose petals showered at Lipa, also on September 15 in 1994. Lipa, Amsterdam and the Jesus King of All Nations Devotion are all concerned with the title of Mary as Mediatrix of All Graces. This shows the links in the chain connecting these four revelations. These images are shown on the inside of the back cover.

Jesus King of All Nations said, "I desire that the souls who embrace My Devotion as 'Jesus, King of All Nations', make a special consecration to My Most Holy Mother under her title of 'Mary,

Mediatrix of All Graces', which it has pleased Me, in My Great Love for her, to give her. People MUST acknowledge her indispensable role as the Mediatrix, the Channel, of all of My Grace to mankind. Only when this dogma is officially proclaimed by My Church, will I truly establish My Reign on earth!" This Consecration is contained in the Appendices.

While we were at Lipa one of the pilgrims who had just finished praying the Devotion's Consecration to Mary, Mediatrix of All Graces, was drawn to a side chapel. When she arrived in the chapel she found that it housed the Lipa statue of Our Lady Mediatrix of All Grace and she was overcome with the aroma of roses that emanated from her! Similarly, many pilgrims smelled the aroma of roses emanating from Teresita.

Our Lady entrusted to Teresita a secret regarding China which she still keeps. She asked us to pray especially for the conversion of China which, she said, will come but only through much suffering.

Similarly, Our Lady told Eda, the Amsterdam visionary, "China will turn to the Mother Church but only after much conflict." And so we left for China and followed the Holy Father's exhortation to "bear witness to the Gospel in the heart of Asia."

Doctor Rosalie Turton with Lipa visionary Teresita prophesying the conversion of China.

12. Shanghai and Beijing, China

Pearl Buck once wrote a short story called "Father Andrea." It was about an Italian missionary priest who had ministered in China for more than a quarter century up to the beginning of the Communist Revolution in the 1920s. He practiced the corporal works of mercy by washing lepers, teaching the Gospel in his mission schoolhouse, reconciling arguments of his peasant parishioners and doing his daily duties. He knew nothing of the gathering storm of the Revolution or its ideology until one day he sought out a runaway student who had joined the Communists.

"In the revolution," his former student said imperiously, "there is no God and there is no duty, we are all free, and we preach a gospel of freedom for everyone." For everyone that is, except those who disagreed with their lies.

Soon thereafter, the Communists came for Father Andrea and one of them announced, "We have come to rid the world of imperialists and capitalists!" These were words which Father Andrea in his simplicity had never heard. The young Communist screamed, "We are the revolutionists! We have come to set everyone free!" With that he shot Father Andrea in the head and he fell to the ground dead.

So began the Chinese Communist Revolution in 1929 with an announcement of freedom but with the reality of oppression through totalitarian terrorism and death. It lasted twenty years and killed millions. Millions more were killed after the Communists came to power in 1949.

Our Lady warned us at Fatima that if her requests were not heeded, "Russia will spread her errors throughout the world, bringing new wars and persecutions of the Church." Her requests were not heeded and so the wars and persecutions came.

Mao Zedong, the leader of the Chinese Communist Revolution, boasted that the greatest Chinese Emperor had only killed 460 intellectuals but that he was responsible for 100 times as many! To him life was cheap. With reference to the possibility of nuclear war he said, "We may lose more than 300 million people. So what? War is war."

From the beginning of the Chinese Communist state in 1949, all religious leaders were ordered to cut ties with foreign churches. Failure to obey resulted in a minimum of 20 years in prison. Churches were taken over by the government and their property was confiscated.

In the 1950's, the government learned that it was easier to control religion than to destroy it. So it established the state-run Patriotic Catholic Church and the state appointed its "bishops." The faithful who remained loyal to the Holy Father became the persecuted Underground Church.

In the 1980's, persecution of the Underground Church increased because of the role of the Church in the downfall of Communism in Eastern Europe and the Soviet Union. Mao never learned, as did Russian Premier Gorbachev, who told the Pope, "The biggest mistake we made was to persecute religion."

At least 20 million innocent Chinese died as the result of Mao's evil Great Leap Forward Program of 1958 by which he tried to instantly create a classless society of equals with no private property. In the year 1958 alone about 700 million Chinese (90% of the population) had their economic, political and administrative life completely transformed.

In one province alone, 5376 agricultural collectives were knocked into 208 large communes with 8000 households in each. These units were expected to be completely self-sufficient even to the extent of producing their own steel! It was a case, as Khrushchev put it, of Mao "acting like a lunatic on a throne and turning his country upside down." Unfortunately, no arrangements had been made by the government to distribute the food crops. They rotted in the fields. People just starved.

Even more evil was Mao's 1966 Great Proletarian Cultural Revolution which destroyed what little cultural goodness and beauty was left in China. Mao welcomed his idolization as a god by the masses of millions of Chinese youth called the Red Guards. Like robots, they memorized and spouted Mao's absurd sayings such as, "From the Red East rises the sun; there appears in China a Mao Zedong" and "The Thought of Mao Zedong must rule and transform the spirit, until the power of the spirit transforms matter!"

At least 100 million people cruelly suffered from roving gangs of violent youths and man-created hell during the Cultural Revolution's ten year period. The Red Guards murdered about 400,000 people! So much for the creation of a heaven on earth by man in opposition to God!

Communism gained support because it offered liberation for the tenant sharecroppers who had been slaves of the landowners. But the Communists took the land from the landowners, re-distributed it by leases to the peasants who then became tenant slaves of the Communist state! The state became the new landowner which then taxed their tenants beyond their ability to pay and left them in dire poverty worse than the old landowners ever had! Through Communist lies and totalitarianism the peasant came full circle back to slavery.

In 1954 Mao Zedong said, "The Soviet Union's today is China's tomorrow." He meant it as a prophecy of Communist progress which, of course, never came. Let us hope that the prophecy is literally true and that Communism in China collapses from its terrorism and repression without bloodshed, as it did in the Soviet Union.

The Chinese Communist rulers are guilty of corruption, graft, bribery, kickbacks and repression. They have no moral authority and exercise their power arbitrarily without the rule of law.

The people have no confidence in their rulers. Despite their new prosperity they are discontented at ruinous taxes, restraints on freedoms of speech, religion and assembly and severe anti-life and anti-family regulations.

For the first time since the Communist Revolution the Triumphant Queen of the World Peace Flight pilgrimage was publicly bringing Jesus and Mary to China. We were completing Rosalie Turton's 1982 pilgrimage to China when she had to leave the statue of Our Lady of Fatima at the border in Hong Kong.

Rosalie had hoped to bring that statue into China with us. So a Chinese woman contacted the Bishop with whom the statue was left in 1982 and asked him to release the statue for China. But the Bishop said that too many miracles had occurred with the statue so she should remain in Hong Kong! However this statue will be in China when Hong Kong becomes a part of China in 1997.

Bishop Cuthbert O'Gara, the missionary to China who died before realizing his hope of sending it a Pilgrim Virgin statue, accompanied us through his personal Chinese Miraculous Medal which had providentially been given to Rosalie shortly before the pilgrimage by a priest friend of his.

We arrived as the largest American charter ever at the Shanghai airport proudly wearing our blue jackets with the Two Hearts insignia, Rosaries around our necks, Jesus and Mary tee shirts and carrying cases with their images on the outside.

Several Chinese pointed to the image of Our Lady of Guadalupe on the Missionary Image case and said, "Maria, Maria!", in recognition of her. I carried a large duffel bag full of religious pamphlets which, with everything else, went straight through customs without any inspection! I guessed that our tourist dollars were worth more to the Chinese than the risk of our evangelizing.

One lady pilgrim went through security wearing her Cross outside her clothing and the Chinese security lady got very excited, reached down inside her blouse, pulled out her Cross and pointed to the pilgrim and said, "Us, us, we are one!"

We expected to see all of the Chinese in Mao suits riding bicycles in an exotic land plastered with signs containing strange Chinese characters. What we saw was quite different!

As we left the Shanghai airport we were greeted by a huge billboard which showed an American cowboy riding a horse and a sign in English which said, "Welcome to Marlboro country"! Nothing could have been more incongruous. No Chinese were wearing Mao suits. All wore Western clothing, most drove cars and most signs were in English!

Metropolitan China is booming with its free market economy. China has adopted free market economic principles within the framework of Communism. It began with President Reagan's promotion of a free market economy and American joint ventures in China. The Chinese are good workers, very diligent, industrious and cheap labor. Private Chinese entrepreneurs are making fortunes. Unfortunately, God is not recognized as their key to happiness. A common advertising sign proclaimed, "Visa (the credit card) is the key to China"!

If China can sustain its economic growth, it will be a great economic miracle and the quickest rise of a population from poverty to a decent standard of living. China's economic growth has averaged 9 percent since the late 1970s. It now ranks third in the economic powers of the world behind America and Japan. It may surpass both within twenty years! This will have earth-shaking global effects on natural resources, the environment, trade and the balance of military power. China is the biggest actor ever in the history of the world stage!

Chinese civil society is now emerging from the cocoon of totalitarianism. It still lacks basic freedoms such as the right to life, freedom of speech, religion and association, public education and government by the rule of law. However, it no longer is totally repressive. Short wave radios and cable television bring in real news from the outside world. Modern communication methods such as fax machines are encouraging the free flow of information. People are starting basic associations such as clubs and labor unions. Educated politicians are replacing peasant politicians and a middle class is slowly forming which demands consumer goods and entertainment rather than propaganda. New books, music and films flourish.

The Chinese government is no longer totalitarian since it doesn't totally control one's life and it doesn't demand one's total allegiance. You needn't support the government so long as you don't oppose it. A fine line to be sure, but a person can hear true news, get an education and print and read books even if he can't use his information and publicly assemble and protest the government. However, China still denies the two fundamental human rights: the right to life and the right to worship God according to one's conscience. We must pray and fast that the persecution of the Church in China ends as it did in Russia so that the people will be free to convert.

Unfortunately, the Chinese really believe that they have religious freedom even while Catholics are being killed and imprisoned. As our tourguide said, "We are free to believe in any religion or not to believe, but most of us choose our freedom not to believe." This is not exactly what we would call an informed choice.

China likes to put on its best face for the world even if it is a false face. I was astounded that all of our tourguides and hotel personnel spoke English. It looked as if English was the language of the people until a tourguide confided to me that they were all educated in English specifically for the tourist industry and that their jobs were compulsory. If they refused to take these jobs they would have no jobs!

China literally presented its false face to the world when it prepared to host the 1990 Asian Games. Along Stadium Road there were many dilapidated houses. In order to make a better presentation to the visiting athletes and leaders, a wall was constructed along the edge of the road to block the view of these houses as you drove down the road. Then they painted the wall to look like a row of new buildings!

As the old Chinese saying goes, "It gleams on the outside - just like donkey droppings." But the inside is something else!

We spent two days in Shanghai going on what were said to be "fifteen minute" bus rides that took three hours each in the busy traffic. We probably prayed more Rosaries over Shanghai than had ever been prayed since the Revolution.

We made a pilgrimage to the National Shrine of Our Lady of Solse, Help of Christians, billed by our tourguide as "the finest in Asia." This shrine, the largest in China, is located on a mountain overlooking Shanghai. Its construction was started in 1900 and completed in 1935. It is run by the Chinese Patriotic Association Church which is not in union with the Holy Father and is controlled by the government which appoints its "bishops."

In May of 1990 mysterious mystical lights began to appear around the National Shrine. Thousands came to view the lights and many cures were claimed in spite of the government's efforts to keep the pilgrims out.

One happy pilgrim here on our pilgrimage was Oda Struver. As soon as she saw the Church, she believed that it was the Church of her parent's marriage in the 1930s. When she saw the steep steps leading to the Church she remembered her mother's story of walking up steep Church steps to be married. Oda met Chinese pilgrim Father Wong on the Church grounds and discovered that he had lived in the same general area as Oda had lived in as a child and they were both familiar with some of the same people and places!

The International Pilgrim Virgin statue of Our Lady of Fatima was crowned as Queen of China at a Mass celebrated in our hotel ballroom. She had waited 45 years from the Communist Revolution for this. A Chinese priest crowned her and led the Act of Consecration of China to the Immaculate Heart of Mary. This was repeated in the hotel in Beijing. These consecrations were made by representatives of the countries of America, Ireland, Australia, China, Philippines and Trinidad.

National Shrine of Our Lady of Solse, Help of Christians, according to tourguide "the finest in Asia."

On our way for departure to Beijing, Fr. Winrich announced that his angel had told him at 2:30 a.m. that this would be a rough day. An understatement! We rose at 3 a.m., onto the bus at 5 with no breakfast for an early arrival at the airport at 5:30 only to find out that it didn't open until 6:30!

We waited outside for one hour and then another hour lounging on the airport terminal floor and the beginning of the Group Visa departure nightmare whereby someone yells out a name in no known order as you listen intently for yours. "Here!", you yell back and you begin to crawl over everyone else and their bags to the check-in line and then off to the gate for another hour's wait.

Pilgrim Chinese priest reading Act of Consecration of China to the Immaculate Heart of Mary.

As we waited for four hours at the Shanghai airport for departure, we noticed the Miracle of the Sun shining through the windows on us and an overwhelming aroma of roses. Our Mother Mary cared. Finally we were off at 11 a.m. Things were looking better but looks are deceiving!

We thought that we would fly from Shanghai to Beijing directly. However as we levelled off, the Captain announced that he had resolved, as he said, "a problem that we have had for some time." The Chinese government had said that we could not fly on our airplane on an *intra-national* flight inside China. We would have to fly to Shanghai on China Airlines. This would have cost us an extra $160,000 so it was decided to outfox the government and fly outside China to Japan and return to China as an *international* flight. "So," said the Captain, "instead of a one hour flight we'll have a five hour flight. I hope that you will be comfortable."

Shortly thereafter we heard a loud bang on the left outside of the airplane which caused a stewardess to jump. We weren't too comfortable. After we touched down in Japan we learned that we had an engine oil filter problem. So we had a longer layover. "But," we thought, "it's all worth it since we've saved ourselves

$160,000 and we've outfoxed the Chinese." But the Chinese had the last word.

Hours later we landed on the tarmac at Beijing only to be told that this was our second entry to China and our Group Visa was only good for a single entry! So we negotiated Chinese style (long and patiently) for three hours in the middle of the night as we sat in the hot airplane without food and they tried to decide what to do with the largest American charter ever to land there.

A pilgrim prayed the Jesus King of All Nations Devotion's Chaplet of Unity to help us get off the plane. Just as she finished it, our exit was announced! The Chinese had finally decided to let us off without a visa for a limited period of 24 hours. Then they confiscated our passports which didn't make us feel too secure. They also restricted us from celebrating any Masses in Chinese churches and from any public religious activities.

The executives from our airline and tourist agency said that they had never encountered so many obstacles with any tourist group and that they hoped they'd never encounter such obstacles again! We overcame all of them with tranquility, peace and calmness although the pilgrims had every reason to complain and rebel. This was the spirit of reparation that Our Lady had requested. The executives were very impressed.

The next day, Father "Bing" had to return to the Philippines and only had one hour to get to the airport when he remembered that his passport had been confiscated. So the accommodating Chinese brought him a sack containing 424 passports! He said a quick prayer, reached in and Voila! he pulled out his passport on the first try. This caused his atheistic tourguide to bless himself in wonderment. It caused us to chant, "Bing-go!"

Unlike Shanghai, where we stood still in traffic, our ten busses were provided with a police escort in the front and the rear as we breezed through the Beijing traffic. This also enabled them to keep a closer eye on us. Our comings and goings in our hotel rooms were monitored by hotel detectives but we fearlessly celebrated Masses in them despite their prohibition.

We travelled to the ancient Great Wall of China which is one of the Seven Wonders of the World. It is almost 1,500 miles long, 20 feet high and 10 feet wide. It is still the longest man-made structure ever built and the only one that is visible from the moon.

We wandered along the meandering Great Wall as illegal aliens while Rosalie and Doctor Courtenay Bartholomew tried to straighten out our visa problem with the American Ambassador and the Chinese authorities.

The Great Wall was built along mountain crests to keep out invaders. It took hundreds of years to build and was finished about 200 B.C. Thousands died building it. One 300 mile section required one million laborers who were torn away from their homes. Half of them were worked to death. There was an average of one death for every yard of the wall that was built. Life is cheap in China.

Cheap enough to kill thousands of innocent peaceful protesting students as the whole world watched. We went to Tiananmen Square and prayed in reparation for the 2,000 students who were killed there in 1989.

Tiananmen means "Gate of Heavenly Peace." There was no earthly peace for the innocent students who died there and hopefully walked through the Gate of Heavenly Peace. No monument marks their sacrifice. No flowers may be left for them and no demonstrations may be made in their memory.

I walked around the entire huge Square and in front of Mao Zedong's tomb located at one end while openly praying the Rosary in reparation for the thousands of killed students and the millions of innocents killed by Mao. After Joseph Stalin's 43 million killed, Mao ranks second in world history with 33 million killed!

An elderly Slovenian lady pilgrim told me that there are really only two kinds of persons. Those for Christ and those against Him. She watched in horror as a 15 year old girl when her Communist neighbors stoned her father to death before her very eyes in front of the Catholic Church. They killed 10,000 Catholics in the neighboring villages in a couple of months. She said it could happen anywhere, anytime now, but that there is nothing to fear. She and her father sang hymns as he died saying, as did Jesus, "Father, forgive them, they don't know what they are doing!"

One of the pilgrims was praying in tongues and a Chinese who overheard her asked her if she spoke Chinese. She answered that she didn't but the Chinese person said, "Yes you do, you just said, 'Thank you God, Thank you Holy Spirit!'"

Another pilgrim had an attack of appendicitis but because she had no passport or visa the tourguides were afraid to take her to the hospital because she might get stranded there. But of all of our pilgrims, this suffering came to the right one because she was Chinese, spoke Chinese and even had relatives in Shanghai! She convinced the tourguides to take her for an emergency operation, her passport was returned to her and she recuperated in Shanghai and returned later to America.

While we were parked outside of a Church, our bus driver and tourguide both witnessed the Miracle of the Sun. The bus driver asked us what it meant and was told that God was blessing him. "God is blessing me!", he shouted in amazement.

We visited the Cathedral of the Immaculate Conception where the pastor told us that 2000 people, mostly youth, attend Sunday services. The wall behind the altar had a beautiful image of Our Lady of All Graces standing on the world as she had appeared to St. Catherine Labouré in Paris in 1830. The Church is maintained by the government - controlled Patriotic Association Church which officially is not in union with the Holy Father.

Here Our Lady appeared to Gianna Sullivan and told her that we were not going to Korea the next day as we had planned but would stay in Beijing an extra day. The next day Our Lady again appeared to Gianna in the Cathedral, identified herself as "Our Lady of All Graces," and said that the mission of our pilgrimage was for the unity of the Church.

Our Lady told Gianna that there were many priests in the Patriotic Church who desire to be loyal to the Holy Father but could not because of government pressure. She then told her that we would all get out of China safely and urged us to remain little and silent allowing God's work to unfold. She invited us all to examine ourselves for self-righteousness. A confirmation of Gianna's message was that in fact we did not go to Korea as we had planned to do.

Pilgrims climbing the Great Wall of China.

"The Doctors"
From left: Doctor Rosalie Turton, Dr. Michael Sullivan, Dr. Gianna Sullivan, and Dr. Courtenay Bartholomew.

Cathedral of the Immaculate Conception with image of Our Lady of All Graces, where Our Lady appeared to Gianna Sullivan.

Official figures list 5.5 million Protestants in China and 3.5 million Patriotic Catholics but the Underground Church of Catholics which is in union with the Holy Father has 12 million! After our Peace Flight was announced, the Chinese government gave greater open encouragement to the Patriotic Church while at the same time increasing its pressure against all those faithful in the Underground Church. "The persecution of the Church today is like an overwhelming storm drowning the world," wrote the Chinese National Conference in a 1994 pastoral letter.

According to figures from the Puebla Institute, a human rights group in Washington, D.C., nearly 180 Christian clergy and religious leaders were arrested between August and December in 1994! We arrived in China in the middle of this persecution.

At least 10 Underground Church leaders were imprisoned indefinitely on August 15, 1994 when the government broke up an annual Assumption Day prayer celebration. Several thousand police troops barricaded the base of a mountain which 2000 Underground Church members were attempting to climb for the celebration. At least half the pilgrims broke through the barricades, but upon reaching the mountain summit they were attacked by police wielding sticks and electric batons. A hundred were injured and the leaders imprisoned.

Two weeks before our arrival in China, Father Gu Zheng was arrested while teaching in an unregistered Roman Catholic seminary. He was imprisoned and the seminary was forcibly closed.

"China's religious persecution has become a masterpiece of deception," said Joseph Kung, nephew of 93-year old Cardinal Ignatius Kung, China's only living Cardinal, and director of the Cardinal Kung Foundation which advocates the rights of Chinese Catholics. "There is constant harassment, but not the long-term sentences" that would provoke international out-cry.

Yet in spite of the government's persecution, conversions are increasing in China. More than 60,000 are baptized each year and thousands celebrate "illegal" Masses.

1994 was a special year for the Chinese Church. It was the seventh centenary of the arrival in 1294 of China's first Bishop, Archbishop Blessed Giovanni da Montecorvino (John of Monte

Corvino). At the time of the Archbishop's death in 1328, he left many churches, convents and schools.

The month before our arrival in China, the Holy Father recalled this celebration and said on the Feast of Our Lady's Nativity, September 8, 1994,

"The celebration of the 7th centenary of Giovanni da Montecorvino's arrival in Beijing offers me the occasion to direct my thoughts to the present Chinese Catholic community....

"I am especially close to those who have remained faithful to Jesus Christ and to His Church in the midst of difficulties of all kinds, and have testified and continue to testify, even at the cost of deep and prolonged suffering, that the principle of communion with the Successor of Peter, whom the Lord constituted His Vicar and the 'permanent and visible source and foundation of unity of faith and fellowship' cannot be renounced by a Catholic who desires to remain such and to be recognized as such. ... Inviting all the sons and daughters of the Catholic Church in China to live this communion in truth and love, my fervent prayer is that it can be manifested in an increasingly visible way."

Regarding the unity of the Church, the Holy Father said in a radio broadcast to the Catholics of China on January 14, 1995,

"Every day I pray for you, asking the Lord to help you to remain united as living members of the one Mystical Body of Christ.

"Unity is not the result of human policies or hidden and mysterious intentions. Instead, unity springs from conversion of the heart, and from sincere acceptance of the unchanging principles laid down by Christ for His Church. Particularly important among these principles is the effective communion of all the parts of the Church with her visible foundation: Peter, the Rock. Consequently, a Catholic who wishes to remain such and to be recognized as such, cannot reject the principle of communion with the Successor of Peter."

In short, the Holy Father is saying to Chinese Patriotic Catholics that if they want to be true Catholics they must be in union with the Pope. While this may seem a severe statement of principle, nevertheless it is the truth.

However, the Holy Father also maintains a benevolent pastoral attitude toward individual Chinese believers. He recognizes that many members of the Patriotic Catholics, including its hierarchy, are in union with the Pope, without being able to say so in public. In 1991, the Holy See acknowledged that the Pope had secretly recognized the legitimacy of about 20 Patriotic Catholic Bishops and many Patriotic priests have pledged loyalty to the Pope. These individuals remain within the Patriotic Association in order to teach the people the true faith.

This explains why the Holy Father told all Chinese Catholics, "I entrust *all* of you to the maternal protection of Mary, Queen of China." It also confirms Our Lady's message to Gianna Sullivan that many Patriotic Catholic priests are in union with the Holy Father.

As a witness of his benevolent attitude, the Holy Father concelebrated Mass in January 1995 with two Patriotic Catholic priests and hundreds of other priests before 4 million people at World Youth Day in the Philippines. The Vatican said that it left the issue of the allegiance to the Pope on "the level of personal conscience." Shi Hongxi, a member of the Patriotic Catholic delegation to World Youth Day said the delegates "regard ourselves as faithful to 'Papa,' so when we see him we regard him also as the highest leader of the Catholic Church."

The Pope also issued a tough diplomatic appeal to China saying that he would acknowledge the Patriotic Association if the Chinese government acknowledged papal authority over the Chinese Catholics of whom he was "well aware of the difficulties amid which you are called to bear witness to your faith in Christ."

It was the second time in just four months that Pope John Paul II had made public statements about China's Underground Church. Having lived under a Communist regime himself in Poland, the Pope very carefully watches the situation of the Church in China. He probably hopes that the Church will peacefully bring about the fall of Communism in China just as it did in Poland and the Soviet Union.

It is not accurate to say that the Patriotic Catholic Association is false and that the Underground Church is true. It is more accurate to say that the former is recognized by the government and is "official" while the latter is not and is "unofficial" or, better yet, that the former has many members in union with the Holy Father while all of the latter are in union with the Holy Father.

It is a confusing situation which demands much patience, firmness, love and determination from the Vatican. To add to the confusion, the Chinese Underground Bishops in their pastoral letter "solemnly declare that the Chinese Catholic Bishops' College (of the Patriotic Catholic Association) and those churches which are led by that College have become a new church. No member of the clergy of the universal Church is permitted to be in communion with them." After all is said and done, only God will judge the conscience of the individual Chinese believer.

One of our pilgrims was a Chinese priest who lived in China until the Communist takeover. He says that those in the Underground Church practice their Baptism as militants for Christ standing up for faith and morals even until death like the early Christians. He says, "Prison is their home, labor camps their parishes and torture their recreation!"

The Underground Church numbers about 12 million and is persecuted because the mere existence of an organized movement not controlled by the Communist Party is construed as a threat to them, especially if it is united to a foreign organization such as the Vatican.

Most of the Underground Church Bishops are in jail with many of the Underground priests. The state-approved Patriotic Bishop Jin of Shanghai dismissed complaints of human-rights violations against Underground priests and said, "They are in jail not because they are priests but because they broke the law."

Because of the few available clergy, the Underground Church is maintained and grows through the laity and their recitation of the Rosary. They say that Our Lady is hiding them from the government by her mantle and they flourish with their prayer groups in the woods, the mountains, the caves and their homes.

Thousands of them make pilgrimages to Our Lady of China Village located only 100 miles from Beijing. There the courageous faithful built two walls, one for Our Lady and one for the Holy Father and they pray in the open at these walls. This is too big for the government to stop.

Since China was opened to foreign contributions in the 1990's, sympathetic Catholics from around the world have contributed almost 5 million dollars. However, all of that money has gone to the Patriotic Catholic Association.

Cardinal Kung, who now lives in America and is the only Chinese Cardinal said, "Unfortunately, many leaders of the universal Church failed to appreciate the heroic practice of faith and fidelity under the continuous persecution in China. Instead of supporting loyal Bishops, many world Bishops and religious communities in the United States and in Europe chose to cooperate with the Patriotic Association."

Our Chinese tourguides were always trying to squeeze as much tourist dollars out of us as possible and continually dropped us at government owned "Friendship Stores" to buy Chinese products.

On our last day they dropped us for three hours! In the store we noticed a gleaming black baby grand piano. What better way to celebrate our departure? So we commandeered it and Father Neil sat down and began to play. About twenty of us gathered around and sang every sing-a-long that we knew, much to the astonishment of the staid Chinese. We sang song after song as they listened in wonderment.

Our tourguide was a student veteran of the Tiananmen Square protests. She was college educated and spoke excellent English. Tourism is the government's number one industry. So the government said that she could become a tourguide or nothing. She's been a tourguide since she graduated from college nine years ago.

She bade us good-bye, "God bless you, God bless you, you're the best group that I've ever had. You are so kind and always smiling. You are, how to say?, warm-hearted and always showing benevolence to the people. Thank you."

Meanwhile, Doctors Rosalie and Courtenay were still trying to straighten out our immigration status with the Chinese and American authorities. We remembered that Our Lady had told Gianna that we would get out of China safely but it didn't look too good.

We had entered China without valid visas. After three hours of wrangling they decided to let us in for a limited grace period of 24 hours and they confiscated our passports. But remember our jet engine trouble? The airport in Beijing couldn't fix it so our plane had to fly to Hong Kong to get a new engine. But, Catch 22, the Chinese wouldn't let the plane leave because the crew didn't have passports or visas which, of course, the Chinese themselves had!

After 13 hours of waiting in the plane, the Chinese finally let the crew fly to Hong Kong. But that delay prevented them from returning to Beijing to fly us out within our 24 hour grace period.

So, Rosalie and Courtenay went to see the American Ambassador to get an extension of our grace period. "This is nuts!" he said. "I couldn't do this for my best friend, so 424 strangers don't have a chance! I've only had one case like this but that was for only one person. You came here with no visa, on an illegal second entry, you're a religious group and there are too many of you. They could keep you here for life!"

But we had Our Lady's promise and many people praying for us. Unbelievably, the Chinese released our sack of passports and we received a 12 hour extension for payment of a $15,000 fee and our agreement that we would not evangelize. So we had until midnight October 28 to get out of town or face a fine of $400 per person, a total of $170,000! But, you guessed it, we had no airplane!

Our trip to Korea was canceled, as Our Lady had prophesied. Would her promise of safely leaving China be fulfilled? Would our airplane get back from Hong Kong on time?

Our airplane got back in the nick of time and we were at the airport by midnight. We brought on the Pilgrim Virgin statue last on the plane at exactly 1:01 a.m. Our Lady was true to her promise and the 101 Flight was ready for take-off to 101 Akita, Japan at 1:01!

A priest had hoped that he could bring a relic of St. Therese of Lisieux, Patroness of Missionaries, to China. In answer to his hope, a pilgrim gave him one and he brought it.

As we left on the airplane from Beijing, the pilgrim told the priest, "Watch out now for St. Therese's sign of roses." Sure enough, our meal was served in a box with two printed red roses on it. Almost 1000 roses in the airplane with us!

My last prayer for the Chinese was,

"Come Holy Spirit and fall upon the Chinese and open their minds and hearts to the knowledge of Jesus Christ. May they acknowledge Him as their Lord, Savior and only Way, Truth and Life. May they stop their anti-life and anti-family policies of coerced contraception, sterilization and abortion. May they have true human development and progress through the generous sharing of our resources and technological knowledge with them so that they can improve their goods and services. May they have true peace, joy, justice and freedoms of life, religion and expression so that the Catholic Church may grow in union with the Holy Father and the Kingdom of God may come to them. Amen!"

Vastness of Tiananmen Square, "Gate of Heavenly Peace", where 2,000 innocent students were brutally killed in 1989.

Pilgrims' jubilant departure from Beijing to Akita.

13. Akita, Japan

We arrived at Akita, Japan as the largest pilgrimage ever to come there. We were greeted warmly by the clergy, faithful and the nuns who displayed "Welcome to Akita" banners.

We toured the beautiful grounds of the Handmaids of the Eucharist where Our Lady had appeared in the 1970s. The outdoor Stations of the Cross were surrounded by an orchard and an adjoining Rosary Garden had a large sculpted statue of Our Lady of Akita in the center. This was surrounded by paths upon which the Rosary could be recited.

The nuns were extremely hospitable and served us tea and coffee as we entered their convent shoeless with our shoes left at the entrance, Japanese style. A great peace pervaded the environment as Sister Agnes, the visionary, greeted pilgrims from her bedroom window. We celebrated a great outdoor Mass.

That evening we all crammed into the tiny guest houses and slept on the floors. One of our priests had lain awake all night unable to sleep and suffering from insomnia. At 2 a.m. another pilgrim insomniac got up for some fresh air. He stumbled over the priest in the dark and the priest asked him to please pray for him because everyone's snoring was driving him nuts and he couldn't take it any more. The pilgrim told the priest that he would go to the Rosary Garden and pray for him to be able to catch some sleep. He did so and returned to find the priest sleeping like a baby.

Later that morning, when he awoke from his reverie, the priest told the pilgrim that he had passed out into the most peaceful sleep that he'd had in years. He asked, "What did you say to Our Lady?" The pilgrim replied, "I looked at the statue of Our Lady of Akita in the garden and said, "Mother, one of your priest sons can't get to sleep and he's at the end of his rope, if you want him to be any good for the rest of us, put him to sleep now!" "And did she ever," the priest replied, "can I call you the next time that I need some sleep?"

Our Lady appeared at Akita to Gianna Sullivan and said, "It is the childlike ways that are the most powerful against evil forces." She told her that our mission had been accomplished in China.

The next day she told Gianna that God allowed the difficulties of the pilgrimage to occur so that each person would see himself in his own spiritual position. She said that God also allowed this because He loves each person so much and that we should rejoice that He had allowed this in order that we would repent and grow in humility.

Our Lady also told her that authentication has nothing to do with how much attention you get or how visible you are in the eyes of man. It has only to do with how you appear in the eyes of God. It has to do with total surrender and quietly working for the Lord for His Glory. We should commit to the Lord our confusion of not knowing, not understanding and not being right and patiently wait for the Spirit to resolve it. For the less the soul works with its own ability, the more securely the journey is because the journey is one of faith.

Our Lady then gave us all the blessing of Akita, the blessing of harmony.

Japanese hosts welcoming pilgrims to Akita.

Sister Agnes Sasagawa, Akita visionary, greeting pilgrims.

PART THREE

War on the Family

14. The Year of the Family

Pope John Paul II proclaimed 1994 as the Year of the Family. He wrote a *Letter to Families* as "a welcome opportunity to knock at the door of your home, eager to greet you with deep affection and to spend time with you." Here are some important excerpts from the Letter.

The family has its origin in that same love with which the Creator embraces the created world. Jesus entered into human history through the family. He fully discloses man to himself beginning with the family in which He chose to be born and to grow up.

Prayer must become the dominant element of the Year of the Family in the Church: prayer by the family, prayer for the family, and prayer with the family.

The family has always been considered as the first and basic expression of man's social nature and the indissoluble character of marriage is the basis of the common good of the family. The family, as a community of persons, is thus the first human society.

There is a certain similarity between the union of the divine persons and the union of God's children in truth and love. Their unity, however, rather than closing them up in themselves, opens them towards a new life, towards a new person, as parents. Begetting is the continuation of Creation. Marriage is a unique communion of persons, and it is on the basis of this communion that the family is called to become a community of persons.

Man is the only creature on earth which God willed for itself. Man cannot fully find himself except through a sincere gift of self. To love means to give and to receive something which can be neither bought nor sold, but only given freely and mutually. The indissolubility of marriage flows in the first place from the very essence of that gift: the gift of one person to another person.

The two dimensions of conjugal union, the unitive and the procreative, cannot be artificially separated without damaging the deepest truth of the conjugal act itself. The logic of the total gift of self to the other involves a potential openness to procreation: in this way the marriage is called to even greater fulfillment as a family.

The person can never be considered a means to an end: above all never a means of pleasure. The person is and must be nothing other than the end of every act. Only then does the action correspond to the true dignity of the person. In the confessional I met difficult cases of rebellion and refusal, but at the same time so many marvelously responsible and generous persons!

The family is fundamental to the civilization of love. Everything contrary to the civilization of love is contrary to the whole truth about man and becomes a threat to him; it does not allow him to find himself and to feel secure, as spouse, parent, or child. So-called "safe sex," which is touted by the "civilization of technology," is actually, in view of the overall requirements of the person, radically not safe, indeed it is extremely dangerous. It endangers both the person and the family. And what is this danger? It is the loss of the truth about one's own self and about the family, together with the risk of a loss of freedom and consequently of a loss of love itself.

The family is the way of the Church. In this letter we wish both to profess and to proclaim this way, which leads to the *kingdom of heaven through conjugal and family life. It is important that the communion of persons in the family should become a preparation for the communion of saints.*

The Church prays that the forces of the civilization of love, which have their source in the love of God, will be triumphant. These are forces which the Church ceaselessly expends for the good of the whole human family.

Jesus appeals to "the beginning," seeing at the very origins of creation God's plan, on which the family is based, and, through the family, the entire history of humanity. What marriage is in nature becomes, by the will of Christ, a true sacrament of the New Covenant, sealed by the blood of Christ the Redeemer. Spouses and families, remember at what price you have been "bought"! See 1 Cor 6:20.

In this way, the Holy Father taught the truth in love about marriage and the family and promoted the culture of life and love. But at the same time the world taught the lie about "free love" and promoted a culture of death.

15. The Attack on the Family

In 1994 the United Nations also proclaimed the International Year of the Family as did the Church. But the world does not teach the truth of the dignity of the human person or God's plan for marriage and the family. It sees persons as objects and marriage and family as options. And so the United Nations promoted artificial contraception, sterilization and abortion and a culture of death. The story is as old as man himself.

Jesus said that from the beginning Satan was a liar and a murderer. He convinced Eve that she had a "choice" which she exercised and which brought death to the world. He instigated Cain to kill his brother Abel which brought death to the human family.

When the Egyptian Pharaoh saw the Israelites multiplying by following God's plan for marriage and the family he said, "Look how numerous and powerful the Israelite people are growing, more so than we ourselves! Come, let us deal shrewdly with them to stop their increase ... if it is a boy, kill him...." Ex 1:9-10, 16. So began population control through killing.

Likewise, in 1974 the United States issued *National Security Study Memorandum 200* regarding implications of worldwide population growth for United States security interests. It recommended population control measures for less developed countries, otherwise they may become more powerful than us. These were the same reasons expressed by the Egyptian Pharaoh thousands of years before!

As the United States population ages and slows in growth because of artificial contraception and abortion, it tries to control the growing populations of the less developed countries of the Third World by the same methods. Through the Agency for International Development billions of dollars have been spent in this attempt. By 1990, one-third of all women of reproductive age in the Dominican Republic and 44% of the women of Brazil had been surgically sterilized!

The 1974 *Memorandum 200* also recommended that the United States "collaborate" with multilateral institutions such as the World Bank and various agencies within the United Nations for the pursuit of its population control goals.

This "collaboration" eventually came to the Philippines with its population control program. When I was there in 1992 with the Missionary Image of Our Lady of Guadalupe, we were greeted by President Ramos at the Filipino White House. I said, "Mr. President I am the ambassador of Our Lady of Guadalupe and on her behalf I beg you not to implement any so-called population control program which promotes the use of artificial contraception because it will lead to abortion as it has throughout the world." This plea fell on deaf ears and the Filipino population control program began.

Two years later, Cardinal Jaime Sin addressed one million Filipinos on August 14, 1994 and accused an "arrogant global dictatorship of imposing a culture of condoms, contraceptives and abortion onto our people." He continued, "We resent the brazen attempts to buy our government and our people - the billions of dollars poured into this deluge of contraceptive drugs and instruments throughout the developing world." "This dictatorship," he said, "would like us to redefine our families and have us ape the degenerate sexual mores prevalent in so-called 'developed' countries."

This "dictatorship" referred to by Cardinal Sin pursued its goals through the United Nations which scheduled an International Conference on Population and Development during its 1994 International Year of the Family. This Conference was heavily influenced by the "collaboration" of international and multilateral agencies and institutions which was recommended in the United State's 1974 *Memorandum 200*.

The Attack on the Family

Ironically, the International Conference on Population and Development was scheduled for Cairo, Egypt where the idea of population control through killing was first expressed by the Egyptian Pharaoh thousands of years before.

Every ten years since 1974 the United Nations has sponsored a conference on population. In 1974 at Bucharest, abortion wasn't even mentioned. In 1984 in Mexico City, abortion was mentioned, but only to *exclude* it from its catalog of family planning methods. But by 1994 the culture of death had progressed to a point where its proponents sought to have abortion declared as an international "human right."

The "Program of Action" proposed for the Cairo Conference included recommendations for world-wide government involvement in family planning through the provision of artificial birth control, sterilization and abortion. It also proposed to recognize different forms of the family such as homosexual unions. Marriage and love weren't even mentioned in the proposal!

The Clinton administration cabled all embassies and ordered all ambassadors to use their influence to push for the anti-family agenda in Cairo. It stated, "The United States believes that access to safe, legal and voluntary abortion is a fundamental right of all women."

On March 18th, the Holy Father had an audience with the Secretary General of the Cairo Conference, Mrs. Nafis Sadik. The Pope expressed his concerns that the Conference proposals would destroy the family unit. He said, "In the face of the so-called culture of death, the family is the heart of the culture of life." "What is at stake here," he told her, "is the very future of humanity." The Holy Father called for proposals which would recognize the dignity of the human person, the truth about marriage and the family and promote human development rather than to prevent or to destroy human life.

On March 19th, the Holy Father wrote to President Clinton and all of the heads of state throughout the world. He said that the Conference proposals "could cause a moral decline resulting in a serious setback for humanity, one in which man himself would be the first victim.... The leaders of the nations owe it to themselves to reflect deeply and in conscience on this aspect of the matter.... What is being held up to the young? A society of 'things' and not of 'persons.' ... Those same people, once they have reached adulthood, will demand an explanation from today's leaders for having deprived them of reasons for living because they failed to teach them the duties incumbent upon being endowed with intelligence and free will."

The Holy Father further commented that the Conference proposals "leave the troubling impression of something being imposed: namely a life-style typical of certain fringes within developed societies which are materially rich and secularized." He then asked, "Are countries more sensitive to the values of nature, morality and religion going to accept such a vision of man and society without protest?"

The Holy Father seemed to imply that the proposals are part of a program of the wealthy nations to keep poorer countries down by controlling their populations rather than to support them through true economic development programs. The Holy Father concluded his letter by noting that "the theme of development ... including the very complex issue of the relationship between population and development, which ought to be at the center of the discussion, is almost completely overlooked."

In April, the Holy Father said, "I have to fight a project conceived by the United Nations which wants to destroy the family. I say simply, 'No, no!' Reflect and be converted.... Aren't there already worrisome symptoms which make us fear for the future of mankind?" He said that "dark forces" threaten the family.

On April 22, the Holy Father personally telephoned President Clinton and requested his intervention to modify the Cairo proposals.

In May, after the Holy Father returned from the hospital, he attributed his suffering in the Year of the Family "because the family is threatened, the family is under attack.

"The Pope has to be attacked, the Pope has to suffer, so that every family and the world may see that there is, I would say, a higher Gospel: the Gospel of suffering by which the future is prepared, the third millennium of families, of every family and of all families.

"... Again I have to meet the powerful of this world and I must speak.

"With what arguments?

"I am left with this subject of suffering. And I want to tell them: understand it, understand why the Pope was in the hospital again, suffering again: understand it, think it over!"

On June 2, while still convalescing from his hip surgery, the Holy Father met personally with President Clinton at the Vatican and urged him not "to be insensitive to the value of life or appear to be advocating policies that would undermine the strength of the family."

It was this courageous witness of truth and suffering by the Pope to the world and his emphatic warnings of the grave threats to the future of the human race and of the family that saved the world from the recognition of abortion as an international "human right" by the United Nations. Such a "right" would have overridden the laws of countries which protected the unborn child and would have been a direct threat to national sovereignties.

At the Cairo Conference Prime Minister Gro Harlem Bruntland of Norway called for a general legalization of abortion. But Pakistani Prime Minister Benazir Bhutto, reflecting Muslim sentiments, said the draft document tries to "impose adultery, sex education ... and abortion" on all countries. "The holy book (Koran) tells us," she said, "Kill not your children on a plea of want. We provide sustenance."

Mother Teresa gave a message to the Conference and said, "I speak today to you from my heart - to each person in all the nations of the world, to people with power to make big decisions.... The greatest destroyer of peace in the world today is abortion.... God has created a world big enough for all the lives He wishes to be born. It is only our hearts that are not big enough to want them and accept them. If all the money that is being spent on finding ways to kill people was used instead to feed them and house them and educate them - how beautiful that would be."

Notwithstanding these pleas, the Cairo Conference went further than any other United Nations conference on population and acknowledged that abortion is legal in most countries and should be made safe. Now governments will be urged to ensure that adolescents be given access to "reproductive health information and care." This can be interpreted to include artificial contraception and abortion. In countries where abortion is not against the law, the declaration implies that health care embraces safe conditions for abortion.

The Vatican stated that it endorsed the Final Document's "recognition of the protection and support required by the basic unit of society, the family founded on marriage." Women's advancement and the improvement of women's status, through education and better health care services were other principles endorsed by the Vatican.

However, the Vatican stated,

"There are other aspects of the Final Document which the Holy See cannot support. Together with so many people around the world, the Holy See affirms that human life begins at the moment of conception. That life must be defended and protected. The Holy See can therefore never condone abortion or policies which favor abortion. The Final Document, as opposed to the earlier documents of the Bucharest and Mexico City Conferences, recognizes abortion as a dimension of population policy and, indeed of primary heath care, even though it does stress that abortion should not be promoted as a means of family planning and urges nations to find alternatives to abortion. The Preamble implies that the Document does not contain the affirmation of a new internationally recognized right to abortion."

For this partial victory, we owe a debt of gratitude to the Pope. In his Christmas Eve talk to the Curia, he stated that the Cairo proposals were "absolutely unacceptable, attempting to include abortion in ambiguous language, among other means of birth control." But, he said, "the Church made its voice heard ... to awaken the consciences." Without his letter to the leaders of the world and the sacrifice of his suffering, abortion may have been recognized as an international "human right." But the danger is not over.

The world's plan is to have abortion declared as an international "human right" and then to declare that no nation can deny this right by its laws. The United Nations would then enforce this "right" world-wide. This would override the national sovereignties of nations whose laws do not permit abortion.

The United Nations could accomplish this by declaring that "unsafe abortion" is an international health problem for women who have a "right" to "reproductive health care." Therefore countries whose laws prohibit abortion make for "unsafe abortions" and thus "endanger reproductive health care" and constitute a violation of "human rights." Such countries would be obligated to allow abortions.

Timothy Wirth, who led the United States delegation at the Cairo Conference summed up this plan when he said, "A government which is violating basic human rights should not hide behind the defense of sovereignty .... Our position is to support reproductive choice including access to safe abortion."

This plan was also evidenced by Joan Dunlop, president of the International Women's Health Coalition who said at the Conference, "The Holy See is in direct confrontation with internationally recognized human rights. It is not a new subject," she insisted, "there have been years of discussion at intergovernmental meetings asserting 'reproductive rights.'"

The United Nations provides a perfect means to implement the world's plan through its international conferences. The United Nations has also recognized that it can increase its influence by expanding the role of non-governmental organizations (NGO's).

These are private organizations such as the International Women's Health Coalition and International Planned Parenthood Federation which promote the world's plan and which have been granted special status by the United Nations to participate in its international conferences in forums and as lobbyists.

The NGO's left Cairo pleased that their concept of "sexual and reproductive rights and health" had been recognized in the Final Document. They are confident that their language and its interpretation will evolve through future conferences into the recognition of an international "human right to abortion."

One month after the Cairo Conference while on our Triumphant Queen of the World pilgrimage, we landed in Cairo to refuel our airplane. As we waited on the tarmac we prayed for the triumph of the culture of life and love and the end of the culture of death.

The International Pilgrim Virgin statue was brought to the opened door to look over Egypt. As we looked out of the airplane many of us saw the Miracle of the Sun and the sun surrounded by a round rainbow. One lady held a small white statue of Our Lady of Fatima towards her window and prayed. Before her very eyes the statue turned into pastel colors of the rainbow! We left with renewed hope.

International Pilgrim Virgin Triumphant Queen overlooking Cairo, Egypt.

16. The Myth of a Population Crisis

All programs which employ artificial contraception, sterilization and abortion as population control methods argue that there is a population problem. Their proponents claim that this causes poverty, starvation, depletion of natural resources, ecological catastrophe and rampant disease. Their solution is to limit and decrease population. Their argument that a lower population growth brings about a faster economic growth has been proved false. In fact, there is no causal connection between the size of a population and the evils that the population alarmists attribute to it such as war, poverty and ecological damage.

A population is composed of human beings and there is no crisis with the number of human beings created by God in His own image and endowed with dignity as His children to whom He said, "Be fruitful and multiply; fill the earth and subdue it." Gn 1:28. The problem is when human beings and governments do not recognize this and treat one another without charity or social justice.

The root cause of poverty and the other evils cited by the population control advocates is not the size of a population but selfishness, a lack of love, mistaken governmental policies and the use of power and resources for ideological purposes such as Joseph Stalin's man-created 1930's famine in the Ukraine which killed millions of innocents. Two-thirds of the people on earth eat less than a bowl of rice per day while a little more than six percent of the world's population in the United States enjoy over 50% of the world's wealth!

There is, or could be with currently available technology, sufficient food, space and natural resources in the world to support any population. The greatest threat to human welfare is not the size of a population. The greatest threat is propaganda of lies and evil methods such as artificial contraception, sterilization and abortion as solutions to a "population crisis" which in fact does not even exist!

As the Holy Father told the Secretary General of the Cairo Conference, Mrs. Nafis Sadik, any population policy must be based on ethical principles. He told her,

"The Holy See seeks to focus attention on certain basic truths; that each and every person - regardless of age, sex, religion or national background - has a dignity and worth that is unconditional and inalienable; that human life itself from conception to natural death is sacred; that human rights are innate and transcend any constitutional order; and that the fundamental unity of the human race demands that everyone be committed to building a community which is free from injustice and which strives to promote and protect the common good. These truths about the human person are the measure of any response to the findings which emerge from the consideration of demographic data."

He also told her that there is a duty to safeguard the family and the liberty of a husband and wife to decide responsibly the number of children that they will have free from all social or legal coercion. Governments should not make these decisions for couples but, rather, should create the social conditions which will enable them to make their own decisions in the light of objective moral criteria. He concluded by saying that "mankind's efforts to respect and conform to God's providential plan is the only way to succeed in building a world of genuine equality, unity and peace."

The Church is the leading institution in the world that celebrates human life itself. It does not urge that couples have unlimited children but that they be free to morally decide for themselves, considering all the circumstances. It hopes that all children will be accepted as gifts from God and supports couples that generously choose to have large families.

17. China:
A Case Study of Population Control

The United Nations Fourth World Conference on Women will be held in 1995 in Beijing, China. This is not an accident but was planned. Many elements of the Chinese population control policy will serve as a model for the international population control proponents. Some of these elements include the setting of national goals or targets, incentives and disincentives for family planning workers and officials, incentives and disincentives for individual families, peer pressure through hostile public opinion, the promotion of provider-controlled, long-term contraceptives, the use of non-governmental organizations (NGO's) to monitor and "persuade" couples, and one-sided promotional propaganda which stresses the existence of a population crisis.

In 1990 the population of China was 1.1 billion or 21.3 percent of the world's total population. In 1973 the central government instituted population control as a basic national policy with limited permissive births, compulsory use by women of intra-uterine devices, abortion and forced sterilization.

In 1979 China implemented a new goal of a limit of one child per family. Premier Deng Xiaoping said, "Use whatever means you must - just do it! With the support of the Chinese Communist Party you will have no problems." And so, without study, planning or proved need, the Chinese Population Control Policy was implemented with a hopeless slogan, "It is better to have more graves than more than one child."

Because a male child maintains the family line and provides economic security for most Chinese, boys are most often desired as the one-child choice. For this reason, unborn girls who are detected by ultra sound are often aborted. Those girl babies who are not aborted are often put up for adoption or are sent to orphanages.

Unfortunately, due to poor care and malnutrition, most of these orphanage babies die before they reach 2 years of age. One study showed that between 1978 and 1985 350,000 Chinese girl babies were killed by their parents or midwives. In the late 1980's ultrasound technology became available in China and abortions of girls gradually replaced infanticide.

The Chinese population control policy is arbitrary and depends on the geographic area. Also the regulations keep changing and are confusing to the millions of peasants who depend on children for help. Generally, all women are required to use intra-uterine devices. After a woman has one child she must be sterilized. This will be forced upon her if she does not have a voluntary sterilization. Second pregnancies are ended by forced abortions. There are local anti-fertility "police" who often surround the home of a woman with a second pregnancy and kidnap her for their "treatment" of a forced abortion.

These police have birth quotas established by the government. If the quotas are met, they are rewarded but if they are exceeded they are punished. So the police have a motive to be ruthless in keeping the birthrate down.

Catholic homes are repeatedly raided by these police, their property is confiscated and pregnant mothers who are unable to escape have abortions and sterilizations forced upon them, even in their last weeks of pregnancy! One hospital administrator admitted to 400 killings at birth by a lethal injection of the crowned head of the baby. "It's like coffee," he said, "at first it's bitter but after a few times you get used to it."

In order to guarantee that they have their preferred boy baby, many pregnant women have an ultrasound to determine the unborn child's sex. If it is a girl, the child is aborted. There are

China: A Case Study of Population Control

more ultrasound machines than any other medical diagnostic equipment in China! By 1990 there were more than 100,000 ultra-sound machines in China.

A Chinese newspaper reported that ultrasound was used in 2,316 cases in one county alone to determine the sex of the unborn child. This resulted in the abortion of 1,006 female children! This has resulted in a disproportionate birth ratio of at least 114 boys born for every 100 girls as compared to the world's natural birth ratio of 105 to 100.

Such a population control policy will have great demographic effects. It will result in a country composed mostly of men who will be unable to find wives. 20 million living Chinese males will not marry for lack of females! This may greatly increase rapes and warfare. History has never experienced such a country with so many males compared to so few females.

Besides limiting the number of children, China has now decided to limit the births of children deemed by them to be "inferior." Xiao Fei, a professor specializing in the mentally handicapped at Beijing Normal University said, "If we can limit the number of these people, the country will shed some of its burden."

The Maternal and Infant Health Care Law of 1995 forbids marriages between those "with certain genetic diseases of a serious nature" (as defined by the state) - unless they agree to sterilization or long-term contraception. The law also requires doctors to "advise" a couple to abort the child if they detect a hereditary disease or an abnormality. For example, couples discovered to have a genetic predisposition toward diabetes could be "advised" to abort their child. This "advice" means coercion in China with its policy of one birth per mother and its history of coercive abortions. This is the beginning of the renewal of the eugenic policies of Nazi Germany.

As we travelled on our pilgrimage throughout Shanghai and Beijing, the two most populous cities in the most populous country of the world, I deliberately looked for pregnant mothers, infants or toddlers. Unbelievably, I saw none of any of them! I looked in the city streets, in the large department stores, in Tiananmen Square, on the Great Wall, in the Temple of Heaven and in the Forbidden City. I saw no pregnant mothers, no infants and no toddlers. The youngest children that I saw were pre-schoolers on outings.

The Chinese one-child policy was very evident. But the Chinese love children! Pilgrim Karen's three children were often embraced by Chinese passerbys but their government had built a modern Great Wall to keep their own children out. This is one of the greatest human rights atrocities in the history of the world.

Where does all this blatant paganism lead to? In 16th century Mexico, human sacrifice led to cannibalism. The witch doctors ate parts of the victims that they killed. Likewise, in China today people eat parts of the aborted fetuses! Human fetuses are the latest health food fad in China.

"They can make your skin smoother, your body stronger, and are good for the kidneys," a doctor at Shenzhen's Sin Hua clinic said, adding that she personally liked her fetuses with pork soup! Staff at the Shenzhen People's hospital which conducted more than 7,000 abortions in 1994, have been selling fetuses for $1.25.

Karen with her three smiling children and the "Ukulele Lady" outside Shanghai Cathedral of Our Lady of Solse, Help of Christians.

18. The Counterattack by Spiritual Warfare

On February 20, 1994, the Holy Father said, "The insidious attacks on the family in modern hedonistic civilization, despite all the declarations on human rights, are essentially opposed to its true good and can only be resisted by prayer, fasting and mutual love .... We trust that (governments) will be able to ... protect the families of ancient societies and nations from this fundamental danger .... Christ says to us ... that this kind of evil is only defeated by prayer and fasting. Yes, there is no other way for us to triumph over this evil, this danger, this threat."

On May 13, 1994, the Holy Father lay in a hospital bed recovering from a hip fracture and replacement. He wrote to the Italian Bishops, "Dear brothers, allow me to think back to what happened 13 years ago in St. Peter's Square.

"We all remember that moment during the afternoon when some pistol shots were fired at the Pope, with the intention of killing him. The bullet that passed through his abdomen is now in the shrine of Fatima ....

"It was a motherly hand that guided the bullet's path, and the agonizing Pope, rushed to the Gemelli Polyclinic, halted at the threshold of death ... (but) the Pope lives - he lives to serve!"

On May 29 he added, "I understood that I must lead Christ's Church into this third millennium by prayer, by various programs, but I saw that this is not enough: she must be led by suffering, by the attack 13 years ago and by this new sacrifice ....

"The Pope has to be attacked, the Pope has to suffer, so that every family and the world may see that there is, I would say, a higher Gospel: the Gospel of suffering by which the future is prepared, the third millennium of families, of every family and of all families."

In this way the Holy Father outlined his counterattack by spiritual warfare upon the culture of death through the supernatural weapons of prayer, fasting, suffering and mutual love.

In 1976 as Cardinal Wojtyla he warned us that "We are standing in the face of the greatest historical confrontation humanity has gone through .... We are now facing the FINAL CONFRONTATION between the Church and the anti-Church, of the Gospel versus the anti-Gospel."

We must realize that Satan exists and that we are not involved in a merely natural battle against human beings but also in a supernatural battle against Satan and the demons in spiritual warfare. St. Paul said, "Our battle is not against human forces but against ... the rulers of this world of darkness, the evil spirits in regions above." Eph 6:12. Jesus said, "This kind does not leave but by prayer and fasting." Mt 17:21.

St. Maximilian Kolbe said that "Modern times are dominated by Satan ... the conflict with hell cannot be engaged by man, even the most clever. The Immaculata alone has from God the promise of victory over Satan. However, assumed into heaven the mother of God now requires our cooperation. She seeks souls who will consecrate themselves entirely to her who will become in her hands effective instruments for the defeat of Satan and the spreading of God's kingdom on earth."

"The Dragon (Satan) became angry with the Woman (Our Lady) and went off to wage war against the rest of her offspring, those who keep God's commandments and bear witness to Jesus." Rev 12:17. Our Lady told Father Gobbi of the Marian Movement of Priests that we are living in this war today. She told him, "I am a Great Sign of battle between me and my Adversary, between the Woman and the Dragon, between my army and the army guided by the enemy of God .... It is necessary that all of you come as quickly as possible to form part of my army. For this, I again invite my children, to consecrate themselves to my Immaculate Heart and to entrust themselves to me as little children."

To help us to realize the reality of Satan, Pope Paul VI said, "Evil is not merely a lack of something, but an affective agent, a living, spiritual being, perverted and perverting, a terrible reality." He said that "one of the greatest needs of the Church today is defense from that evil which is called the devil."

Pope Leo XIII recognized this need of defense from the devil in the nineteenth century after he had a mystical vision of the satanic evil to come in this twentieth century. He composed a battle prayer to St. Michael the Archangel and sent it to all of the Bishops of the world.

On April 24, 1995, Pope John Paul II said that Pope Leo XIII certainly had a very vivid recollection of the great apocalyptic battle of Chapter 12 of the Book of Revelation when he composed the prayer to St. Michael. He said that the Woman Clothed With the Sun referred to in Revelation is Our Lady. He said that "when all threats against life gather before the Woman who is about to give birth, we must turn to the Woman Clothed With the Sun, so that with her motherly care, she may protect every human being threatened in his mother's womb .... May prayer strengthen us for the spiritual battle .... The Book of Revelation refers to this same battle, recalling before our eyes the image of Saint Michael the Archangel (Rev 12:7)." The Holy Father then led the prayer composed by Pope Leo XIII,

"Saint Michael the Archangel, defend us in battle; be our protection against the wickedness and snares of the devil. May God rebuke him, we humbly pray. And do thou, O prince of the heavenly host, by the power of God, cast into hell Satan and all the evil spirits who prowl about the world seeking the ruin of souls. Amen."

The Pope concluded, "Although today this prayer is no longer recited at the end of Mass, I ask everyone not to forget it, and to recite it to obtain help in the battle against the forces of darkness and against the spirit of this world."

In the Jesus King of All Nations Devotion, St. Michael revealed how Jesus wished the holy Archangel to appear with Him on a medal. It was revealed that around the border of the medal should appear the words from the Book of Daniel, "At that time their shall arise Michael, the Great Prince, Guardian of Your People." Dn 12:1. An ejaculation was also revealed, "St. Michael, Great Prince and Guardian of your people, come with the holy angels and saints and protect us!"

St. Michael also revealed that it was the most holy will of God that he be honored as the Protector of the Church of Christ on Earth and Guardian of the Most Blessed Sacrament. He said, "I promise to those souls who embrace this Devotion and invoke me under my title of Protector of the Church of Christ on Earth, protection from the enemy during life and especially at the hour of their ... death when the assaults of the enemy are most violent."

St. Michael the Archangel carrying banner of Our Lady of Guadalupe and defeating Satan. See Rev 12:7-8.

AT THAT TIME THERE SHALL ARISE MICHAEL, THE GREAT PRINCE, GUARDIAN OF YOUR PEOPLE

PROTECT US!

Image of St. Michael the Archangel revealed as part of the Jesus King of All Nations Devotion with the title, "Protector of the Church of Christ on Earth and Guardian of the Most Blessed Sacrament." See Dn 12:1.

19. The Counterattack by The International Holy Family Year Congress

While we were on the Triumphant Queen of the World pilgrimage we attended The International Holy Year Family Congress in the Philippines with over one thousand participants including eighteen Bishops.

In the keynote address Bishop Pedro Dean said that by confronting the evil proposals of the Cairo Conference, "The Church has once more made itself a sign of contradiction, like Our Lord Jesus Christ - preaching a way that is less than easy, but which is the only true way toward a real human development." He concluded by saying, "Let me end this opening address with a fervent prayer to the Holy Family, a model for all families, that through our meditation and discussion these days, we may be able to draw positive lessons and resolutions from the recent events surrounding the Cairo Conference, so that like the plains periodically flooded by the Nile, we too may rise stronger and better equipped to work for the family towards the civilization of love."

One of our pilgrims, Dr. Courtenay Bartholomew of Trinidad, also addressed the Congress. Dr. Bartholomew is a research scientist who was part of the original team to isolate the HIV virus in 1984. With reference to the AIDS epidemic he said, "Unfortunately, in the absence of any cure to date, we are now witnessing a 'manic' response. Know the word 'mania' means a mental derangement, a madness. This type of mania I call 'condomania.' It is supposedly man's solution to the epidemic, not God's. There is a virus, a retro-virus, let loose in this world, which in my opinion is a missionary virus. It is a virus with a mission and a message. A message which is still not being heeded after 13 years of its scientific discovery. This message of the virus is certainly not about condoms. It is only the feeble minded who would not recognize the message of the virus, which is about chastity before marriage and fidelity afterwards. Chastity is the only cure to the AIDS epidemic."

The Congress debated and approved four major sets of resolutions which built upon previous congresses held in Russia, Japan, Kenya, Venezuela, Australia, the United States and the Caribbean. These resolutions were in the areas of Family Life, the Alliance of the Two Hearts of Jesus and Mary, St. Joseph and the Communion of Reparation.

In the area of Family Life, the Congress resolved that the Christian family must be open to and respect human life at every stage and should erect home altars dedicated to the Holy Family for Scripture readings, Rosary and consecration to the Two Hearts. Families should also practice natural family planning, evangelize their neighbors regarding the Church teachings on family life and stand up for life against the culture of death.

In the area of the Alliance of the Two Hearts, the Congress resolved that we enter the Alliance of the Two Hearts, live our Total Consecration, be an expression of lay spirituality that revitalizes the Sacrament of Marriage and reinforces the family as a domestic church and enthrone the image of the Two Hearts in our homes.

In the area of St. Joseph, the Congress resolved that increased devotion to him as the Protector and Guardian of Christian families should be fostered with emphasis on his sublime dignity as father of the Holy Family and the model for entering the Alliance of the Two Hearts. Fathers should also lead family prayer and worship, assume responsibility at home, observe spousal fidelity and provide direction and unity in the family.

In the area of the Communion of Reparation, the Congress resolved that we should commit ourselves to the practice of the Communion of Reparation during First Friday and First Saturday by reciting the Rosary, receiving the sacraments of Confession and Eucharist and adoring the Blessed Sacrament all with the intention of making reparation for the sins of the world.

From the time that we left Fatima on our pilgrimage, we had carried a statue of the Holy Family with us. This statue was specially created for our pilgrimage by the artist Carlos Ayala. The statue showed Our Lady holding the child Jesus with St. Joseph looking over her shoulder. It represented them in their finest clothing at the time of the Presentation of the Child Jesus in the temple. Because of the significance of the International Holy Family Year Congress we left the Holy Family statue as a gift for the organizers.

Statue of Holy Family at International Holy Family Year Congress.

PART FOUR

The Final Dogma

20. The Alliance of the Two Hearts

At Fatima, Jesus told Sister Lucia that He wished "to put the devotion to the Immaculate Heart beside the devotion to my Sacred Heart." This began the devotion to the Alliance of the Two Hearts.

The International Holy Family Year Congress which we attended in the Philippines was dedicated to the Alliance of the Two Hearts.

"The Alliance of the Two Hearts" is a term first used by Pope John Paul II in his Angelus Address of September 15, 1985 when he said,

"When the side of Christ was pierced with the centurion's lance, Simeon's prophecy was fulfilled in her: 'And a sword will pierce through your own soul, also.' Lk 2:35.

"The words of the prophet are a foretelling of the definitive alliance of these hearts: of the Son and of the Mother; of the Mother and of the Son. 'Heart of Jesus, in whom dwells all the fullness of the divinity.' Heart of Mary - Heart of the sorrowful Virgin - Heart of the Mother of God!

"May our prayer of the Angelus, unite us today with that admirable alliance of hearts."

These hearts are the Sacred Heart of Jesus and the Immaculate Heart of Mary. These Hearts are not just biological organs but symbols of the centers of their persons, their whole beings; their interior lives, thoughts, wills and sentiments.

In the Angelus we pray the words of the angel Gabriel's Annunciation to Mary, "Behold the handmaid of the Lord, be it done unto me according to thy word." Lk 1:38.

It is this "Yes" said by Our Lady that began the Alliance of the Two Hearts. At that precise moment the Sacred Heart of Jesus began to beat beneath the Immaculate Heart of Mary through the working of the Holy Spirit. We should repeat our personal "yes" to God's will as we discern it in our lives in order to unite our hearts to the Alliance of these Two Hearts.

On June 9, 1985 the Holy Father said, "Through the Immaculate Heart of Mary, let us remain in the Covenant with the Heart of Jesus." An alliance is entered into by an agreement or covenant. Mary entered into the covenant with the Heart of Jesus at the Annunciation by her "Yes" and she cooperated with God's plan for our redemption throughout her life until Calvary when her Immaculate Heart was pierced simultaneously with the Sacred Heart of her Son. That is why she is called our Co-Redemptrix or Co-Operator with Jesus in His plan of Redemption.

We can enter this covenant by imitating Mary, becoming co-redeemers with her and uniting ourselves with "this admirable Alliance of Hearts," to which the Holy Father referred, by our Total Consecration to the Sacred Heart of Jesus through the Immaculate Heart of Mary. By this Consecration we repeat our Baptismal commitment to renounce Satan in union with these Hearts.

In this way, as the Holy Father said on April 12, 1985, we collaborate "with Christ the Redeemer through the offering of (our) own lives united and lived with the Heart of Christ in Total Consecration to His love and in reparation for the sins of the world, through the Immaculate Heart of Mary Most Holy."

In the Holy Father's Act of Consecration of the World he said, "Consecrating ourselves to Mary means accepting her help to offer ourselves and the whole of mankind to Him who is Holy, infinitely Holy; it means accepting her help - by having recourse to her motherly Heart, which beneath the Cross was opened to love for every human being, for the whole world - in order to offer the world, the individual human being, mankind as a whole, and all the nations, to Him who is infinitely Holy."

So our primary response to the love of the Heart of Jesus is our consecration and reparation. By our consecration we repay

Christ's love by our love in return. By our reparation we make up for the world's insults to His love.

The reparative practices of our union with the Alliance of the Two Hearts are at least monthly Confession and the Communion of reparation which Our Lady requested at Fatima. We should also adore Jesus in the Blessed Sacrament, pray the daily Rosary and make the Morning Offering of all our prayers, works, joys and sufferings in union with the Holy Sacrifice of the Mass throughout the world.

At Fatima the Angel appeared before the children with a chalice and a Host suspended above it shedding blood into the chalice in mid-air. He prostrated himself before Jesus really present in the Blessed Sacrament and prayed,

"O Most Holy Trinity, Father, Son and Holy Spirit, I adore Thee profoundly. I offer Thee the Most Precious Body, Blood, Soul and Divinity of Jesus Christ, present in all the tabernacles of the world, in reparation for the outrages, sacrileges and indifference by which He is offended. By the infinite merits of the Sacred Heart of Jesus and the Immaculate Heart of Mary, I beg the conversion of poor sinners."

Similarly, Jesus revealed a prayer to Blessed Faustina Kowalska as a part of His Chaplet of Mercy,

"Eternal Father, I offer You the Body and Blood, Soul and Divinity of Your dearly beloved Son, Our Lord Jesus Christ in atonement for our sins and those of the whole world."

Likewise, Our Lady approved the following Eucharistic Prayer at Akita,

"Most Sacred Heart of Jesus, TRULY present in the Holy Eucharist, I consecrate my body and soul to be entirely one with Your Heart, being sacrificed at every instant on all the altars of the world and giving praise to the Father, pleading for the coming of His Kingdom.

"Please receive this humble offering of myself. Use me as You will for the glory of the Father and the salvation of souls.

"Most Holy Mother of God, never let me be separated from Your Divine Son. Please defend and protect me as Your special child. Amen."

Finally, Jesus revealed in the Jesus King of All Nations Devotion a request and a promise regarding His reception with love in Holy Communion,

"Let them offer me, within their very souls, through my Immaculate Mother to my heavenly Father, who will then smile down upon them benevolently and who will grant these souls His Fatherly blessing."

These are the reparative prayers and acts which have been revealed as most pleasing to the Alliance of the Two Hearts.

Our pilgrimage uniform was a blue jacket with the logo of the Alliance of the Two Hearts. This logo is shown at the end of this chapter. It shows the offering of our heart to the Two Hearts, surrounded by the Rosary and the Brown Scapular all of which is overshadowed by the Holy Spirit. It contains the motto, "Unus In Sui Amore" which is Latin for "One in Their Hearts."

The logo shows the Sacred Heart of Jesus as the offering of His Heart for us. It shows the Immaculate Heart of Mary in Alliance with the Sacred Heart by accepting His love through her "Yes" at the Annunciation. It shows the offering of our heart in imitation of St. Joseph to the Alliance of the Two Hearts by our Total Consecration to Jesus through Mary.

The logo is surrounded by the Brown Scapular which is the sign of our Total Consecration and the Rosary which we pray daily as Our Lady requested. All of this is overshadowed by a dove which represents the Holy Spirit which overshadowed Our Lady at the Annunciation and formed the Sacred Heart beneath her Immaculate Heart. This is the same Spirit which overshadowed Our Lady and the apostles at Pentecost and He who will come to us in the New Pentecost.

Logo of the Alliance of the Two Hearts.

21. Mary, Mediatrix of All Graces

On our 1992 pilgrimage to Russia, we visited Rue du Bac, Paris. Our Lady appeared there to St. Catherine Labouré in 1830 and revealed the Miraculous Medal. She also appeared standing on the globe. In her hands she held a smaller globe with a tiny Cross at the top. She held it up as an offering to God, with her eyes raised heavenward and her lips praying for the whole world.

Rays of light streamed from gems on her fingers and fell upon the large globe. Our Lady told St. Catherine, "The rays are the graces which I give to those who ask for them." This apparition symbolized her role as the Mediatrix of All Graces.

Jesus said, "I desire that the souls who embrace my devotion as 'Jesus King of All Nations', make a special consecration to my most holy Mother under her title of 'Mary, Mediatrix of All Graces', which it has pleased me, in my great love for her, to give her." This consecration is contained in the Appendices.

Jesus continued, "People MUST acknowledge her indispensable role as the Mediatrix, the Channel, of all of my grace to mankind. Only when this dogma is officially proclaimed by my Church, will I truly establish my reign on earth!"

Grace is the very life of God which is communicated to us from the Father and is merited for us by the Son who offered Himself as a ransom for us as the one and only mediator between

God and men. See 1 Tim 2:5-6. A mediator is a friendly third party who interposes between parties who are not united. Jesus is our mediator with God because He shared our human nature so that we could share His divine nature through the graces merited by His passion and death.

Such mediation does not exclude a subordinate mediation by Our Lady between Jesus and us through her intercession and dispensation of the graces merited by Him. As Jesus is our mediator with God the Father of our redemption, Mary is our Mediatrix with God the Son of His graces.

These graces are mediated from Jesus to us by Mary, Mediatrix of All Graces who is His Mother and ours. This is a natural consequence of her divine motherhood. It is simply the will of Almighty God to exercise the power of Christ's mediation by the application of His merited graces to us through the mediation of His Mother.

The title of Mediatrix of All Graces befits Our Lady's dignity because she did such great things for our salvation as a participant with her Son in His redemption, furnishing Him with a body and sharing His sufferings right up to His crucifixion.

Jesus makes her a continuing participant in His redemption by placing her in charge of His merits to be distributed by her to us. In this way she frees sinners, enriches the needy, elevates the just and affords a universal refuge to all men.

St. Louis de Montfort said, "To go to Jesus, we must go to Mary; she is our mediatrix of intercession. To go to God the Father, we must go to Jesus; for He is our mediator of redemption."

Our Lady's role as Mediatrix of All Graces was foreshadowed at the wedding feast at Cana where she interceded with Jesus and mediated His gift of new wine. See Jn 2. Similarly, Our Lady as Mother of the Church obtains for us the spiritual nourishment of all graces necessary for our eternal salvation. The mystery of her mystical maternity first foreshadowed at the Annunciation, then at Cana and finally at the crucifixion is now carried out in her role as Mediatrix of All Graces.

Mary, Mediatrix of All Graces

Pope John Paul said in his encyclical, *Mother of the Redeemer*, "Mary places herself between her Son and mankind in the reality of their wants, needs and sufferings. She puts herself 'in the middle,' that is to say she acts as a mediatrix not as an outsider, but in her position as Mother. She knows that as such she can point out to her Son the needs of mankind, and in fact, she 'has the right' to do so."

On our 1994 pilgrimage to China we saw the image of St. Catherine Labouré's apparition on the wall behind the altar of the Cathedral of the Immaculate Conception in Beijing, China. We also saw that this image is the same image as the statue of Our Lady of Lipa in the Philippines and the same image as the statue of Our Lady of Akita in Japan who stands before the cross. This statue in turn is the same image as the image of Our Lady of All Nations who appeared in Amsterdam to a Dutch woman named Eda from 1945 to 1959. These images are shown on the inside of the back cover.

In Amsterdam Our Lady revealed that the final Marian dogma to be proclaimed will define her as "Co-Redemptrix, Mediatrix and Advocate." Our Lady revealed that she requested that this title be proclaimed, "Because she has been sent by her Lord and Creator in order, through this title and this prayer (contained in the Appendices) to preserve the world from a universal disaster."

All of these images from Rue du Bac, Amsterdam, Lipa and Akita are associated with Our Lady's title as "Mediatrix of All Graces." Finally, in 1990 Our Lady revealed the image of "Jesus Christ Mediator, Our Lady Mediatrix of All Graces" which sums up the meaning of all of the preceding images.

The Cross in the images symbolizes Our Lady's continuing role as Co-Redemptrix. This title means that Our Lady shared with Jesus in His plan for our redemption. She gave birth to the Redeemer and shared in His sufferings until she stood at the foot of His Cross.

The images show Our Lady standing on the earth with the Cross behind her. The images teach us that God the Father "so loved the world that He gave His only Son." Jn 3:16. The Son in turn gave to His Father His very self (see Lk 23:46), consecrated Himself for our sake (see Jn 17:19) and gave to us His Body and Blood (see Lk 22:19-20) and the Holy Spirit. See Jn 20:22.

The images show that Mary stood near the Cross (see Jn 19:25) from which Jesus gave her to us and us to her. See Jn 19:26. From this holy sacrifice and Our Lady's mediation, grace and mercy come to us. She begs us for our consecration and reparation in return.

PART FIVE

The Triumphant Queen of Peace

22. Warnings and Chastisements

Jesus King of All Nations said, "I AM King of Heaven and earth! Hear Me, O peoples of the earth! My Reign is near at hand. Turn from your perverse and evil ways! I tell you, unless you turn back to Me and repent, My judgment will come upon the earth ....

"No, My beloved, sin and the evils committed by mankind are too great, no longer will I spare My judgment to correct the conscience of mankind as a whole ...." However, He promised that each time we pray the devotional prayers He would "mitigate the chastisements upon your country."

God never inflicts chastisements without warning us through His servants, the prophets. "Whoever is dear to me I reprove and chastise. Be earnest about it, therefore. Repent!" Rev 3:19.

God's love for His sinful children is shown through the prophets who issue warnings to us to turn back to God and pray and fast for peace or suffer chastisements. History shows that heeding the call to repentance is critical.

Jonah warned Nineveh of its destruction but the people repented, prayed, fasted, and lived in peace. On the contrary, Jesus warned Jerusalem of its destruction but the people did not listen and Jerusalem was annihilated. Jesus prophesied that not a stone upon a stone would be left in Jerusalem because they did not recognize the path to peace. See Lk 19:41-44. This prophecy was literally fulfilled in the year 70 A.D. by the Roman General Titus who destroyed the city.

In these latter days, God has sent us as His prophets His Mother and the Holy Father, Pope John Paul II. Our Lady appeared at Fatima in 1917 and warned us to turn to God and to stop offending Him. She said that if her wishes were not fulfilled "certain nations will be annihilated."

Because so few responded to Our Lady's requests made at Fatima, she appeared to Sister Agnes at Akita, Japan on October 13 1973, the anniversary of her last apparition at Fatima, and told her, "If men do not repent and better themselves, the Father will inflict a terrible punishment on all humanity. It will be a punishment greater than the deluge, such as one will never have seen before. Fire will fall from the sky and will wipe out a great part of humanity, the good as well as the bad, sparing neither priests nor faithful. The survivors will find themselves so desolate that they will envy the dead. The only arms which will remain for you will be the Rosary and the Sign left by my Son. Each day recite the prayers of the Rosary. With the Rosary, pray for the Pope, the Bishops and the priests."

Bishop Ito, the Bishop of Akita, said, "It seems to me that Our Heavenly Father needs to purify this corrupt world before allowing mankind to enter the 21st century. The Blessed Mother appears to ask for souls who will offer up their fervent prayers, sacrifices, and sufferings to God in order to contribute to the realization of God's Kingdom of Justice and Love."

St. Peter said that the godless "deliberately ignore the fact that the heavens existed of old and earth was formed out of water and through water by the word of God; through these the world that then existed was destroyed, deluged with water. The present heavens and earth have been reserved by the same word for fire, kept for the day of judgment and of destruction of the godless." 2 Pt 3:5-7.

But the righteous and devout shall be preserved. "He rescued Lot, a righteous man oppressed by the licentious conduct of unprincipled people .... The Lord knows how to rescue the devout from trial and to keep the unrighteous under punishment for the day of judgment ...." 2 Pet 2:4-9.

Chastisements from God are acts of His love for the good of our eternal salvation. Our Lady is the prophetess of the coming Chastisement. She comes in love for all of her earthly children to warn us so that we might be able to do something about it.

Our Lady told Father Stefano Gobbi of the Marian Movement of Priests that the purpose of the Chastisement is the purification and renewal of the world and the salvation of souls. It will be the worst chastisement in the history of the world but will result in a new Pentecost.

Jesus will live again in the hearts of humanity and through us He will act, work, love, suffer, die and rise to a new life in His Church so that He will "present to Himself a glorious Church, holy and immaculate, without stain or wrinkle or anything of that sort." Eph 5:27. Jesus will reign in a universal reign of grace, of beauty, of harmony, of communion, of sanctity, and of justice and peace.

Knowing this, our attitude towards the future Chastisement should be one of hope. We shouldn't think about chastisements because we may enter into them. Our responsibility is to accept divine peace and to live it.

Fear of the Chastisement is useless, what is needed is trust. "We should have confidence on the day of judgment ...." 1 Jn 4:17. Our Lady told Sister Agnes, "I alone am able still to save you from the calamities that approach. Those who place their confidence in me will be saved."

Excessive curiosity regarding the prophesied Chastisement should be replaced by confidence and obedience to Our Lady's requests for prayer, penance and consecration to her Immaculate Heart.

For example, too many are curious to learn the contents of the so-called "Third Secret of Fatima" which was sent by Sister Lucia to the Vatican and was expected to be revealed in 1960. Since then, Popes have read it but in the exercise of their prudential judgment have not publicly revealed it.

Sister Lucia said that the Third Secret was never meant for the ordinary faithful but only for the Pope himself. She said, "The Pope can reveal it if he chooses to, but I advise him not to. If he chooses to, I advise great prudence."

Pope John Paul II sought to stifle excessive curiosity about the Third Secret and to encourage us to heed Our Lady's requests. He said, "If there is a message in which it is said that the oceans will flood entire sections of the earth; that, from one moment to the other, millions of people will perish ... there is no longer any point in really wanting to publish this secret message.

"Many want to know merely out of curiosity, or because of their taste for sensationalism, but they forget that 'to know' implies for them a responsibility. It is dangerous to want to satisfy one's curiosity only, if one is convinced that we can do nothing against a catastrophe that has been predicted .... (At this point the Holy Father took hold of his Rosary and said,) Here is the remedy against all evil! Pray, pray and ask for nothing else. Put everything in the hands of the Mother of God!

"We must be prepared to undergo great trials in the not-too-distant future; trials that will require us to be ready to give up even our lives, and a total gift of self to Christ and for Christ. Through your prayers and mine, it is possible to alleviate this tribulation, but it is no longer possible to avert it, because it is only in this way that the Church can be effectively renewed."

One alleviation of this tribulation was the avoidance of a nuclear war which Sister Lucia stated "would have occurred in 1985" if the Holy Father had not made the Collegial Consecration of the World on March 24, 1984!

Another alleviation of this tribulation occurred through the Jesus King of All Nations Devotion. Jesus spared Puerto Rico from a devastating seaquake which their sins justly deserved because, He said, "some have received me as their Lord and King in the Devotion that I have given you to give to the world, that of 'Jesus, King of All Nations.' My message was received with an open heart and with an open soul and they did not receive you with scorn or indifference or mock the messages that I have sent, or refuse to listen!

"I have shown them that if they turn to me, their Merciful King who desires to reign in their hearts, that I am a King of Mercy, a Father of Mercy, a Lord of Love who does not want their unnecessary deaths and condemnation of their souls because of their sins and stubbornness in pride.

"Have no doubt! The thunder of my justice was going to be heard! As thunder comes before the rain so the thunder of my just judgment upon them was going to be heard first! Will my children WAKE UP and see the lightning first? The lightning of the merciful rays of my Mercy that I wish to strike their hearts with!

"Will they notice me who AM? Will my people finally see with the light of my grace so that I can reign in their hearts? Yes, I wish to be the Light that comes before the reign! The reign of my Merciful Kingship! Choose my people, choose how you wish to serve me!

"It is you my special little ones who have found the fulfillment of my promises not only for yourselves, but for your whole nation! Remember what I have done for you my people, of how I have spared you this time!"

23. The Triumph of the Immaculate Heart of Mary and the Era of Peace

The Triumph of the Immaculate Heart of Mary was first announced by Our Lady at Fatima on July 13, 1917 when she told the children, "In the end, my Immaculate Heart will triumph. The Holy Father will consecrate Russia to me and she will be converted, and an era of peace will be granted to the world."

A scriptural analogy for the triumph of the Immaculate Heart of Mary is the Book of Esther. Queen Esther interceded before the King and prevented the annihilation of the Jewish people which had been scheduled for the thirteenth day of the month.

Likewise, Our Lady interceded before her son Jesus King of All Nations to prevent the annihilation of nations and always appeared at Fatima on the thirteenth day of the month. "Esther" means "star" and when Our Lady appeared at Fatima she wore a star on her dress which suggests the analogy.

Esther was a Jewish Queen married to King Xerxes of Persia in the fifth century before Christ. Haman was the King's highest official. He prevailed upon the King to order that all of the King's servants would kneel and bow down to Haman. Queen Esther's servant, Mordecai, refused to render this homage to Haman because he would not render to man the homage which he regarded as belonging to God alone.

This refusal enraged Haman to such an extent that he plotted vengeance not only upon Mordecai but upon all of the Jewish people. He told the King that the Jews obeyed their own laws but not those of the King. He prevailed upon the King to issue a decree that all Jewish men, women and children should be annihilated on the same day, the thirteenth day of the month.

A law of Persia provided that no one, not even the Queen, could enter the King's court without an invitation and that anyone who did so would suffer the automatic penalty of death, unless the King extended the golden scepter of his mercy. Esther had not been invited to the King's court. Nevertheless, she decided to pray and fast with her people for three days and then go for an audience with the King to intercede for the salvation of her people. She bravely said, "If I perish, I perish!" Esther 4:16.

She prayed, "My Lord, our King, you alone are God. Help me, who am alone and have no help but you, for I am taking my life in my hand. ... O God, more powerful than all, hear the voice of those in despair. Save us from the power of the wicked, and deliver me from my fear." Esther C:14-15; 29.

Esther entered the King's presence glowing with the perfection of her beauty. Her countenance was joyful and lovely even though she was filled with fear. The King was seated on his throne in all his majesty. He was clothed in full robes and covered with gold and precious stones. He inspired great awe. He looked at his wife in majestic anger for having entered without his invitation and was about to issue an order for her death when Esther suddenly fainted.

God melted the King's heart and changed his anger to gentleness. He raised the golden scepter of his mercy, touched her with it and saved her from death. He also promised her that whatever she requested of him would be granted. Esther requested that he spare the lives of the Jewish people who had been unjustly condemned to annihilation through the evil plan of Haman.

Haman had built a gibbet upon which to hang Mordecai and to begin the annihilation of the Jews on the thirteenth day of the month. When the King learned all of this he ordered that Haman himself should be hung on that gibbet and that on the thirteenth day of the month the Jews were to be granted religious freedom. On that day the Jews destroyed all of their enemies.

The Triumph of the Immaculate Heart of Mary and the Era of Peace

So the evil plan of Haman and his followers for the annihilation of the Jews was reversed and came back upon their own heads by God's merciful love.

Mordecai replaced Haman and he and Esther worked for the welfare of their people. This day is still celebrated by the Jewish people as the feast of Purim. It celebrates their deliverance through the triumph of Queen Esther and her period of peace.

The Book of Esther is an analogy to the Triumph of the Immaculate Heart of Mary because Satan (Haman) has plotted the annihilation of nations which Our Lady (Queen Esther) prophesied as a possibility at Fatima.

To prevent this Our Lady requested the First Saturday Devotion just as Queen Esther prayed and fasted with her people. Our Lady intercedes to God for us pleading for mercy to prevent the annihilation just as Queen Esther did with the King. Because of her intercession God will grant us His mercy, prevent the annihilation and grant us the period of peace just as the King did for Queen Esther. This will be the Triumph of the Immaculate Heart of Mary our Queen just as it was the triumph of Queen Esther.

This Triumph of the Immaculate Heart of Mary, the prevention of annihilation and her promised period of peace began with the Holy Father's collegial consecration of the world to her Immaculate Heart on March 25, 1984 and is an ongoing process.

Sister Lucia said that the Triumph of the Immaculate Heart of Mary "refers to the errors that were being spread by Russia .... Our Lady's Immaculate Heart triumphed over the errors that were being spread by Communist Russia."

Sister Lucia also said that Our Lady's prophecy at Fatima of a possible "annihilation of nations" was prevented by the Holy Father's Consecration because "The Consecration of 1984 prevented a nuclear war that would have occurred in 1985." She went on to say, "The period of peace does not refer to civil peace but rather to a peace that we are now living with the end of the spread of the errors of Communist Russia." Our Lady had prophesied at Fatima that these errors would spread if we did not respond to her requests.

Finally, now that we are in "the end" that Our Lady prophesied at Fatima, her remaining promises will be fulfilled: "My

Immaculate Heart will triumph, the Holy Father will consecrate Russia to me and she will be converted, and a period of peace will be granted to the world."

Jesus King of All Nations told His servant, "My most holy Mother is preparing the great triumph. The triumph of her Immaculate Heart ushers in the reign of my love and mercy. I will extend to them the golden scepter of my mercy (like Queen Esther's King, Xerxes), so that they may be received by me, through my most holy Mother."

As Sister Lucia said, Our Lady's prophesied period of peace does not refer to civil peace. This peace is not merely the absence of external conflict. It is a positive interior quality which is a gift from Jesus (see Jn 14:27) beginning in our hearts and flowing like a river to our family, neighbors and society, gathering them all in its current. St. Augustine said that "our hearts are ever restless Lord until they rest in thee." Only then will we experience God's own peace which is beyond all understanding. See Phil 4:7.

This peace is not obtainable by any human peace program. Jesus said that "without me you can do nothing." Jn 15:5. Peace is a gift from God that cannot be earned by our effort, imposed by political effort or gained by any human means whatsoever. This peace is not obtainable without responding to Our Lady's requests of conversion, faith, prayer and fasting.

With this peace, we pray with Pope John Paul II who visited the Basilica of Our Lady of Guadalupe and prayed to her, "Thus most holy Mother, with the peace of God in our conscience, with our hearts free from evil and hatred we will be able to bring to all true joy and true peace, which comes to us from your Son, our Lord Jesus Christ, who with God the Father and the Holy Spirit lives and reigns for ever and ever. Amen."

24. The New Evangelization and the Great Jubilee Year 2000

Perhaps the greatest program of the pontificate of Pope John Paul II is his New Evangelization and the Great Jubilee Year 2000. Since the publication of the very first document of his pontificate, he has spoken explicitly of the Great Jubilee and suggested that the time leading up to it be lived as a "New Advent." In a series of addresses since 1988 he said,

"We are approaching the Third Millennium! Therefore, I want to call on you once again, as apostles of a New Evangelization, to help build the civilization of love.

"From the First Pentecost onward, the Holy Spirit has been working in the life and history of mankind. He is at work in the world, which is approaching the Third Christian Millennium, in order to make it the Kingdom of love of the Father.

"With full confidence let us place under the vigilant intercession of Holy Mary the passage to the year 2000 and the prospect of the Third Millennium. The Third Millennium remains for us a horizon of very stimulating reflections, because it makes us look forward in hope. The Blessed Mary is the guide in the new exodus towards the future.

"May Mary be the model to which the People of God look in order to live out their missionary commitment. Let us ask her with trust to intercede with her Son to obtain for the Church a New

Pentecost, a new Missionary Advent for the Jubilee Year 2000 and for the beginning of the Third Millennium of the Christian faith.

"God is preparing a great new springtime for humanity.

"The Year 2000 is the most important anniversary that humanity has ever known."

In 1994 as the Third Millennium drew near, the Holy Father published his apostolic Letter *Tertio Millennio Adveniente* on Preparation for the Great Jubilee Year 2000. He said that Our Lady's motherhood "will be felt during this year as a loving and urgent invitation addressed to all the children of God, so that they will return to the house of the Father."

He also said that the great challenge of the year 2000 "certainly involves a special grace of the Lord for His Church and for the whole of humanity."

In his apostolic letter the Holy Father has set forth a plan of preparation for the Great Jubilee divided into two phases, the first three years as a general preparation and the last three years as an immediate preparation for the 2000th commemoration of the Birth of Jesus Christ. This Jubilee, like biblical jubilees is a "day blessed by the Lord" and thus a time of joy.

"The Jubilee celebration should confirm the Christians of today in their *faith* in God who has revealed Himself in Christ, sustain their *hope* which reaches out in expectation of eternal life and rekindle their *charity* in active service to their brothers and sisters."

To cross the threshold of the new millennium we must examine ourselves and purify ourselves, through repentance and acknowledge the weaknesses of the past. We must also implore the Holy Spirit for the grace of Christian unity. "It is essential not only to continue along the path of dialogue on doctrinal matters, but above all to be more committed to prayer for Christian unity: 'Father that they also may all be one in us'. Jn 17:21."

The second phase of the immediate preparation will take place from 1997 to 1999 with a Trinitarian thematic structure. 1997 will be devoted to reflection on Christ, the Word of God, with renewed emphasis on the Bible and a renewed appreciation of Baptism and the virtue of faith through a detailed study of the *Catechism of the Catholic Church.*

The Blessed Mother will be contemplated in this first year especially in the mystery of her Divine Motherhood and as a model of faith which is put into practice.

1998 will be dedicated in a particular way to the Holy Spirit with renewed appreciation of His presence and His activity towards Christian unity and in the Sacrament of Confirmation. The virtue of hope will be aimed at "the definitive coming of the Kingdom of God."

The Blessed Mother "will be contemplated and imitated during this year as the woman who was docile to the voice of the Spirit, a woman of silence and attentiveness, a woman of hope who, like Abraham, accepted God's will 'hoping against hope'."

1999, the third and final year of preparation, will be aimed at the perspective of the Father. Emphasis will be placed on conversion from sin and towards good and a renewed appreciation of the Sacrament of Penance, and the virtue of charity with a "greater emphasis on the Church's preferential option for the poor and the outcast."

In the tradition of the biblical jubilee celebrations which forgave debts, the Holy Father proposes that the Great Jubilee will be a good time to give thought "to reducing substantially, if not canceling outright, the international debt which seriously threatens the future of many nations." Interreligious dialogue especially with the Jews and Muslims should have a pre-eminent place. The crisis of our civilization "must be countered by the civilization of love, founded on the universal values of peace, solidarity, justice and liberty, which find their full attainment in Christ." The Blessed Mother will be contemplated as the perfect model of love towards both God and neighbor.

The phase of the actual celebration of the Great Jubilee Year 2000 will be aimed at the glorification of the Trinity. "In this sense the Jubilee celebration makes present in an anticipatory way the goal and fulfillment of the life of each Christian and of the whole Church in the Triune God."

The year 2000 will be intensely Eucharistic with emphasis on the Sacrament of the Eucharist and the celebration of an International Eucharistic Congress in Rome.

The whole responsibility for the celebration of the Jubilee was entrusted by the Holy Father to "Mary, Mother of the Redeemer. She, the Mother of Fairest Love, will be for Christians on the way to the Great Jubilee of the Third Millennium the Star which safely guides their steps to the Lord."

So we should pray with hope as Jesus taught us, "Thy Kingdom come!" Amen.

The Triumphant Queen of the World

QUEEN OF THE WORLD

Holy Father consecrating the world to Our Lady before original statue of Our Lady of Fatima, March 25, 1984.

QUEEN OF RUSSIA

International Pilgrim Virgin statue crowned by Russian youth, Lena, and Bishop Paulo Hnilica in Red Square, Moscow, October 1992.

QUEEN OF CHINA

International Pilgrim Virgin statue crowned by Chinese priest in Shanghai, October 1994.

Our Lady of Guadalupe
The Triumphant River of Light

Monsignor Guillermo Shulenburg, Abbot of the Basilica Shrine of Our Lady of Guadalupe in Mexico City, prayed upon the blessing of the Missionary Image at the Basilica Shrine that "the Missionary Image of Our Lady of Guadalupe be a River of Light on her Journey." He expressed his hope that Our Lady of Guadalupe would "fulfill the prophecy of Pope John Paul II that the Basilica will be a center 'from which the light of the Gospel of Christ will shine out over the whole world by means of the Miraculous Image of His Mother'."

The word Guadalupe in Spanish means "River of Light." The image on the opposite page depicts Our Lady of Guadalupe as The River of Light. This painting is a visual representation of the spiritual role of Our Lady of Guadalupe. It portrays her as the victorious Woman who crushes Satan, the serpent, in fulfillment of the promise of the Book of Genesis. (See Gn 3:15).

This painting was done by a nun who saw a vision of it appear next to film maker John Bird while he gave a talk on Our Lady of Guadalupe.

We see Our Lady as the Triumphant River of Light, surrounded by the angel of suffering and the angel of adoration, standing within a vertical column of light over a river. She and the river have toppled and crushed the column of the stone serpent idol and replaced it at Tepeyac with the column of the Joyful Mysteries of the Rosary.

"The people who walked in darkness have seen a great light; upon those who dwelt in the land of gloom a light has shown. You have brought them abundant joy and great rejoicing, . . . for the yoke that burdened them, the pole on their shoulder, and the rod of their taskmaster you have smashed . . ." Is 9:1-3.

The power of God, the light of the Holy Trinity, shines through Mary and destroys the kingdom of Satan. Our Lady of Guadalupe mediated this light to the pagan Aztecs who dwelt in darkness. She brought them abundant joy and great rejoicing. She smashed the stone serpent idol and the yoke of human sacrifice that burdened them.

Our Lady of Guadalupe stands in the painting at the center of the columns from left to right representing El Bethel, Zaragoza, Guadalupe and Tepeyac.

The River of Light flows from its source at El Bethel, where Jacob the patriarch built the first temple in the world to God, to Zaragoza, Spain, where St. James built the first Christian temple in the world. From there it climbs up to the Shrine of Guadalupe in the mountains of Spain. At last it comes to the Temple at Tepeyac in Mexico, precisely at the midpoint of the Americas, bringing peace and joy to those who come with an open heart to visit Our Lady of Guadalupe.

We recall the joyful prayer of Pope John Paul II upon his visit to the Basilica Shrine of Our Lady of Guadalupe, the River of Light, "Thus most holy Mother, with the peace of God in our conscience, with our hearts free from evil and hatred we will be able to bring to all true joy and true peace, which comes to us from your Son, our Lord Jesus Christ, who with God the Father and the Holy Spirit lives and reigns for ever and ever. Amen."

The Triumphant King of All Nations

Image of Jesus King of All Nations overlooking 2 million Filipino faithful.

25. Epilogue: The Homecoming

Our pilgrimage left Akita, Japan, anxiously looking forward to our homecoming to New York City. Since there were a few Californians on the airplane we had scheduled a "quick stop" in Anchorage, Alaska so that they would have a short connecting flight home.

We arrived in Anchorage at 3 a.m. and, since it was our first re-entry to the United States, we had to pass through Customs. This necessitated the off-loading of all of our baggage.

Unfortunately, there were only three baggage men to do this. More unfortunately, their mechanical cargo net broke as soon as they started working. So they had to offload and re-load the baggage of over 400 passengers by hand! This took 6 1/2 hours as we patiently waited while Our Lady received our last ounces of suffering.

As we left the terminal at 9:30 a.m., we received Our Lady's "send-off" as we witnessed the Miracle of the Sun rising with shimmers and dances over the beautiful mountains.

We landed in New York at 9:30 p.m. having travelled around the world by air a grand total of 48 hours and 48 minutes over a distance of 24,407 miles. Our Lady had just one more night to squeeze out from us our last bit of penance. She made the best of it. We arrived in New York too late to make our scheduled connecting flights!

I escorted Karen and her three children as we bussed with all of our luggage to our connecting terminal where we planned to sleep on the floor together. But, par for the course, as soon as we arrived the terminal closed down for the night!

So we trudged off to the main terminal seeking rest. All kinds of strange people passed by us with no security in sight. So we prudently left to find a hotel. Being professional "waiting people" by this time, an hour's wait for a bus at 12:30 a.m. was easy! We arrived safely at our hotel for a 1 a.m. bed time; Karen went up to her room and I wearily asked the clerk for a 5 a.m. wakeup call. What else should I have expected?

As my head hit the pillow, the airplane captain's farewell to us echoed in my ears, "We wholeheartedly bid you peace and wish you a good night!"

Appendices

A. The Fatima Messages 143

B. The Fatima Prayers 145

C. The Akita Messages and Prayer 147

D. The Amsterdam Message and Prayer 149

E. St. Louis' Act of Total Consecration 151

F. Pope John Paul II's Act of Consecration of the World.... 153

G. Consecration to Mary, Mediatrix of All Graces from the Jesus King of All Nations Devotion 157

APPENDIX A

THE FATIMA MESSAGES

May

Will you offer yourselves to God, and bear all the sufferings He sends you in atonement for all the sins that offend Him and for the conversion of sinners? ... The grace of God will be with you and will strengthen you. Say the Rosary every day to bring peace to the world and an end to the war (World War I).

June

Continue saying the Rosary every day. And after each of the mysteries, I want you to pray in this way: O my Jesus, forgive us our sins; save us from the fires of hell; lead all souls to heaven, especially those in most need of your mercy .... Jesus wishes you (Sister Lucia) to make me known and loved on earth. He wishes also for you to establish devotion in the world to my Immaculate Heart. (This is the first Fatima secret, revealed in 1927.) I will be with you always, and my Immaculate Heart will be your comfort and the way which will lead you to God.

July

Continue to say the Rosary every day in honor of Our Lady of the Rosary, to obtain the peace of the world and the end of the war, because only she can obtain it. In October I will tell you who I am. I will then perform a miracle so that all may believe. (Following is the second Fatima secret, revealed by Sister Lucia in 1940:) Make sacrifices for sinners, and say often, especially while making a sacrifice: O Jesus, this is for love of Thee, for the conversion of sinners, and in reparation for offenses committed against the Immaculate Heart of Mary. (The children are shown hell.) You have seen hell, where the souls of sinners go. It is to save them that God wants to establish in the world devotion to my Immaculate Heart. If you do what I tell you, many souls will be saved, and there will be peace. This war will end, but if men do not refrain from offending God, another and more terrible war will begin (World War II). To prevent this, I shall come to the world to ask that Russia be consecrated to my Immaculate Heart, and I shall ask that on the First Saturday of every month Communions of reparation be made in atonement for the sins of the world. If my wishes are fulfilled, Russia will be converted and there will be peace; if not, then Russia will spread her errors throughout the world, bringing new wars and persecution of the Church; the good will be martyred and the Holy Father will have much to suffer; certain nations will be annihilated. But in the end, my Immaculate Heart will triumph. The Holy Father will consecrate Russia to me and she will be converted, and the world will enjoy a period of peace .... (The third secret follows.)

August

Continue to say the Rosary every day. In October ... St. Joseph will come with the holy Child to bring peace to the world. Our Lord will come to bless the people. Our Lady of the Rosary and Our Lady of Dolors will also come at that time. Make sacrifices for sinners. Many souls go to hell because no one is willing to help them with sacrifice.

September

Continue the Rosary. Say it every day that the war may end. (Here Our Lady repeated all she had said in August, and added Our Lady of Mount Carmel to those who would appear in October.) God is pleased with your sacrifices ....

October

I am the Lady of the Rosary. I want a chapel built here in my honor. Continue saying the Rosary every day. The war will end soon .... Some petitions I will grant, others I must deny. People must amend their lives and ask pardon for their sins. They must not offend Our Lord any more, for He is already too much offended. There is nothing more. (Then, while the miracle of the sun took place for all present to see, the children beheld the visions promised in the preceding apparitions.)

APPENDIX B

THE FATIMA PRAYERS

Angel Prayer

While the Blessed Sacrament was suspended in the air, the Angel prostrated himself before it and recited this prayer:

O Most Holy Trinity, Father, Son and Holy Spirit, I adore you profoundly. I offer you the Most Precious Body, Blood, Soul and Divinity of Jesus Christ, present in all the tabernacles of the world, in reparation for the outrages, sacrileges and indifference by which He is offended. By the infinite merits of the Sacred Heart of Jesus and the Immaculate Heart of Mary, I beg the conversion of poor sinners.

Eucharistic Prayer

This prayer stresses the most beautiful truth that the all-powerful, all-loving God is present in the Blessed Sacrament:

O Most Holy Trinity, I adore You! My God, my God, I love You in the Most Blessed Sacrament.

Rosary Decade Prayer

Our Lady asked that this prayer be recited after each decade of the Rosary:

O my Jesus, forgive us our sins; save us from the fires of hell; lead all souls to heaven, especially those in most need of your mercy.

Pardon Prayer

This was the first prayer the angel taught the children. He repeated these words three times, then rose and said, "Pray thus. The Hearts of Jesus and Mary are attentive to the voice of your supplications."

O my God, I believe, I adore, I trust and love You! I beg pardon for all those who do not believe, do not adore, do not trust and do not love You.

Sacrifice Prayer

Our Lady taught the children this prayer to be said when they would have something to sacrifice to God.

O my Jesus, it is for love of You, in reparation for the offenses committed against the Immaculate Heart of Mary, and for the conversion of poor sinners.

APPENDIX C

THE AKITA MESSAGES AND PRAYER

<u>First Message</u>

My daughter, my novice, you have obeyed me well in abandoning all to follow me. Is the infirmity of your ears painful? Your deafness will be healed, be sure. Be patient. It is the last trial. Does the wound of your hand cause you to suffer? Pray in reparation for the sins of men. Each person in this community is my irreplaceable daughter. Do you say well the prayer of the Handmaids of the Eucharist? Then, let us pray it together.

(Then Our Lady prayed with Sister Agnes the prayer of the Handmaids of the Eucharist:) Most Sacred Heart of Jesus, truly present in Holy Eucharist, I consecrate my body and soul to be entirely one with Your Heart, being sacrificed at every instant on all the altars of the world and giving praise to the Father pleading for the coming of His Kingdom.

Please receive this humble offering of myself. Use me as You will for the glory of the Father and the salvation of souls.

Most Holy Mother of God, never let me be separated from your Divine Son. Please defend and protect me as your special child. Amen.

(When the prayer was finished, Our Lady said:)

Pray very much for the Pope, Bishops and priests. Since your Baptism you have always prayed faithfully for them. Continue to pray very much ... very much.

<u>Second Message</u>

My daughter, my novice, do you love the Lord? If you love the Lord, listen to what I have to say to you.

It is very important. You will convey it to your superior.

Many men in this world afflict the Lord. I desire souls to console Him to soften the anger of the Heavenly Father. I wish, with my Son, for souls who will repair by their suffering and their poverty for the sinners and ingrates.

In order that the world might know His anger, the Heavenly Father is preparing to inflict a great chastisement on all mankind. With my Son I have intervened so many times to appease the wrath of the Father. I have prevented the coming of calamities by offering Him the sufferings of the Son on the Cross, His Precious Blood, and beloved souls who console Him forming a cohort of victim souls. Prayer, penance and courageous sacrifices can soften the Father's anger. I desire this also from your community ... that it love poverty, that it sanctify itself and pray in reparation for the ingratitude and outrages of so many men. Recite the prayer of the Handmaids of the Eucharist with awareness of its meaning; put it into practice; offer in reparation whatever God may send for sins. Let each one endeavor, according to capacity and position, to offer herself entirely to the Lord.

Even in a secular institute prayer is necessary. Already souls who wish to pray are on the way to being gathered together. Without attaching too much attention to the form, be faithful and fervent in prayer to console the Master.

<u>Third Message</u>

As I told you, if men do not repent and better themselves, the Father will inflict a terrible punishment on all humanity. It will be a punishment greater than the deluge, such as one will never have seen before. Fire will fall from the sky and will wipe out a great part of humanity, the good as well as the bad, sparing neither priests nor faithful. The survivors will find themselves so desolate that they will envy the dead. The only arms which will remain for you will be the Rosary and the Sign left by my Son. Each day recite the prayers of the Rosary. With the Rosary, pray for the Pope, the Bishops and the priests.

The works of the devil will infiltrate even into the Church in such a way that one will see Cardinals opposing Cardinals, Bishops against other Bishops. The priests who venerate me will be scorned and opposed by their confreres ... churches and altars sacked; the Church will be full of those who accept compromises and the demon will press many priests and consecrated souls to leave the service of the Lord.

The demon will be especially implacable against souls consecrated to God. The thought of the loss of so many souls is the cause of my sadness. If sins increase in number and gravity, there will be no longer pardon for them.

Pray very much the prayers of the Rosary. I alone am able still to save you from the calamities which approach. Those who place their confidence in me will be saved.

APPENDIX D

THE AMSTERDAM MESSAGE AND PRAYER

<u>Message</u>

Our Lady said, "I come as Co-Redemptrix-Mediatrix at this time. Co-Redemptrix I was already at the Annunciation. This means that the Mother became Co-Redemptrix by will of the Father. Tell your theologians this. Tell them moreover, that this will be the last dogma in Marian history. This picture shall prepare the way."

<u>Prayer</u>

Lord Jesus Christ, Son of the Father, send now your Spirit over the earth. Let the Holy Spirit live in the hearts of all peoples, that they may be preserved from corruption, disaster and war. May the Lady of All Peoples, who once was Mary, be our Advocate! Amen.

APPENDIX E

ST. LOUIS' ACT OF TOTAL CONSECRATION

Consecration to Jesus Christ,
the Incarnate Wisdom,
through the Blessed Virgin Mary

O Eternal and Incarnate Wisdom! O sweetest and most adorable Jesus! True God and true man, only Son of the Eternal Father, and of Mary, always Virgin! I adore Thee profoundly in the bosom and splendors of Thy Father during eternity; and I adore Thee also in the virginal bosom of Mary, Thy most worthy Mother, in the time of Thine Incarnation.

I give Thee thanks for that Thou hast annihilated Thyself, taking the form of a slave in order to rescue me from the cruel slavery of the devil. I praise and glorify Thee for that Thou has been pleased to submit Thyself to Mary, Thy holy Mother, in all things, in order to make me Thy faithful slave through her. But, alas! Ungrateful and faithless as I have been, I have not kept the promises which I made so solemnly to Thee in my Baptism; I have not fulfilled my obligations; I do not deserve to be called Thy child, nor yet Thy slave; and as there is nothing in me which does not merit Thine anger and Thy repulse, I dare not come by myself before Thy most holy and august Majesty. It is on this account that I have recourse to the intercession of Thy most holy Mother, whom Thou has given me for a mediatrix with Thee. It is through her that I hope to obtain of Thee contrition, the pardon of my sins, and the acquisition and preservation of wisdom.

Hail, then, O Immaculate Mary, living tabernacle of the Divinity, where the Eternal Wisdom willed to be hidden and to be adored by angels and by men! Hail, O Queen of Heaven and earth, to whose empire everything is subject which is under God. Hail, O sure refuge of sinners, whose mercy fails no one. Hear the desires which I have of the Divine Wisdom; and for that end receive the vows and offerings which in my lowliness I present to thee.

I (Name), a faithless sinner, renew and ratify today in thy hands the vows of my Baptism; I renounce forever Satan, his pomps and works; and I give myself entirely to Jesus Christ, the Incarnate Wisdom, to carry my cross after Him all the days of my life, and to be more faithful to Him than I have ever been before.

In the presence of all the heavenly court I choose thee this day for my Mother and Mistress. I deliver and consecrate to thee, as thy slave, my body and soul, my goods, both interior and exterior, and even the value of all my good actions, past, present and future; leaving to thee the entire and full right of disposing of me, and all that belongs to me, without exception, according to thy good pleasure, for the greater glory of God, in time and in eternity.

Receive, O benignant Virgin, this little offering of my slavery, in honor of, and in union with, that subjection which the Eternal Wisdom deigned to have to thy maternity, in homage to the power which both of you have over this poor sinner, and in thanksgiving for the privileges with which the Holy Trinity has favored thee. I declare that I wish henceforth, as thy true slave, to seek thy honor and to obey thee in all things.

O admirable Mother, present me to thy dear Son as His eternal slave, so that as He has redeemed me by thee, by thee He may receive me! O Mother of mercy, grant me the grace to obtain the true Wisdom of God; and for that end receive me among those who thou lovest and teachest, whom thou leadest, nourishest and protectest as thy children and thy slaves.

O faithful Virgin, make me in all things so perfect a disciple, imitator and slave of the Incarnate Wisdom, Jesus Christ thy Son, that I may attain, by thine intercession and by thine example, to the fullness of His age on earth and of His glory in Heaven. Amen.

APPENDIX F

POPE JOHN PAUL II'S ACT OF CONSECRATION OF THE WORLD

"We have recourse to your protection, holy Mother of God."

As we utter the words of this antiphon with which the Church of Christ has prayed for centuries, we find ourselves today before you, Mother, in the Jubilee Year of the Redemption.

We find ourselves united with all the Pastors of the Church in a particular bond whereby we constitute a body and a college, just as by Christ's wish the Apostles constituted a body and college with Peter.

In the bond of this union, we utter the words of the present Act, in which we wish to include, once more, the Church's hopes and anxieties for the modern world.

Forty years ago and again ten years later, your servant Pope Pius XII, having before his eyes the painful experiences of the human family, entrusted and consecrated to your Immaculate Heart the whole world, especially the peoples for which by reason of their situation you have particular love and solicitude.

This world of individuals and nations we too have before our eyes today: the world of the second millennium that is drawing to a close, the modern world, our world!

The Church, mindful of the Lord's words: "Go ... and make disciples of all nations ... and lo, I am with you always, to the close of the age" (Mt 28:19-20), has, at the Second Vatican Council, given fresh life to her awareness of her mission in this world.

And therefore, O Mother of individuals and peoples, you who know all their sufferings and their hopes, you who have a mother's awareness of all the struggles between good and evil, between light and darkness, which afflict the modern world, accept the cry which we, moved by the Holy Spirit, address directly to your Heart. Embrace, with the love of the Mother and Handmaid of the Lord, this human world of ours, which we entrust and consecrate to you, for we are full of concern for the earthly and eternal destiny of individuals and peoples.

In a special way we entrust and consecrate to you those individuals and nations which particularly need to be thus entrusted and consecrated.

"We have recourse to your protection, holy Mother of God": despise not our petitions in our necessities.

Behold, as we stand before you, Mother of Christ, before your Immaculate Heart, we desire, together with the whole Church, to unite ourselves with the consecration which, for love of us, your Son made of himself to the Father: "For their sake," he said, "I consecrate myself that they also may be consecrated in the truth" (Jn 17:19). We wish to unite ourselves with our Redeemer in this his consecration for the world and for the human race, which, in his divine Heart, has the power to obtain pardon and to secure reparation.

The power of this consecration lasts for all time and embraces all individuals, peoples and nations. It overcomes every evil that the spirit of darkness is able to awaken, and has in fact awakened in our times, in the heart of man and in his history.

How deeply we feel the need for the consecration of humanity and the world — our modern world — in union with Christ himself! For the redeeming work of Christ must be shared in by the world through the Church.

The present Year of the Redemption shows this: the special Jubilee of the whole Church.

Above all creatures, may you be blessed, you, the Handmaid of the Lord, who in the fullest way obeyed the divine call!

Hail to you, who are wholly united to the redeeming consecration of your Son!

Mother of the Church! Enlighten the People of God along the paths of faith, hope and love! Help us to live in the truth of the consecration of Christ for the entire human family of the modern world.

Pope John Paul II's Act of Consecration of the World

In entrusting to you, O Mother, the world, all individuals and peoples, we also entrust to you this very consecration of the world, placing it in your motherly Heart.

Immaculate Heart! Help us to conquer the menace of evil, which so easily takes root in the hearts of the people of today, and whose immeasurable effects already weigh down upon our modern world and seem to block the paths towards the future!

From famine and war, deliver us.

From nuclear war, from incalculable self-destruction, from every kind of war, deliver us.

From sins against the life of man from its very beginning, deliver us.

From hatred and from the demeaning of the dignity of the children of God, deliver us.

From every kind of injustice in the life of society, both national and international, deliver us.

From readiness to trample on the commandments of God, deliver us.

From attempts to stifle in human hearts the very truth of God, deliver us.

From the loss of awareness of good and evil, deliver us.

From sins against the Holy Spirit, deliver us, deliver us.

Accept, O Mother of Christ, this cry laden with the sufferings of all individual human beings, laden with the sufferings of whole societies.

Help us with the power of the Holy Spirit to conquer all sin; individual sin and the "sin of the world", sin in all its manifestations.

Let there be revealed, once more, in the history of the world the infinite saving power of the Redemption; the power of merciful Love! May it put a stop to evil! May it transform consciences! May your Immaculate Heart reveal for all the light of Hope!

APPENDIX G

CONSECRATION TO MARY, MEDIATRIX OF ALL GRACES FROM JESUS KING OF ALL NATIONS DEVOTION

O Mary, Most Holy and Immaculate Mother of God, of Jesus, our Victim-High Priest, True Prophet, and Sovereign King, I come to you as the Mediatrix of All Graces, for that is truly what you are. O Fountain of all Grace! O Fairest of Roses! Most Pure spring! Unsullied Channel of all of God's grace! Receive me, Most Holy Mother! Present me and my every need to the Most Holy Trinity! That having been made pure and holy in His Sight through your hands, they may return to me, through you, as graces and blessing. I give and consecrate myself to you, Mary, Mediatrix of All Graces, that Jesus, our One True Mediator, Who is the King of All Nations, may Reign in every heart. Amen.

BIBLIOGRAPHY

Akita, the Tears and Messages of Mary: Teiji Yasuda, translated by John M. Haffert (101 Foundation, Asbury, New Jersey, 1989).

China Wakes: Nicholas D. Kristof and Sheryl Wudunn (Times Books, New York, New York, 1994).

Fatima in Lucia's Own Words: Fr. Louis Kondor, Editor (The Ravengate Press, Cambridge, Massachusetts, 1976).

Finally Russia!: John M. Haffert (101 Foundation, Asbury, New Jersey, 1993).

Lipa: June Keithley (Cacho Publishing House, Manila, Philippines, 1992).

Mankind's Final Destiny: Howard Q. Dee (Assisi Development Foundation, Manila, Philippines, 1993).

Modern Times: Paul Johnson (Harper Collins Publishers, New York, New York, 1991).

Our Lady of Guadalupe and Her Missionary Image: Daniel J. Lynch (The Missionary Image of Our Lady of Guadalupe, St. Albans, Vermont, 1993).

People Power, The Philippine Revolution of 1986: Monina Allarey Mercado, Editor (Writers and Readers Publishing, New York, New York, 1986).

The Call to Total Consecration to the Immaculate Heart of Mary: Daniel J. Lynch (The Missionary Image of Our Lady of Guadalupe, St. Albans, Vermont, 1991).

The Cause of Liberation in the USSR: Rene Laurentin (Queenship Publishing, Santa Barbara, California, 1993).

The Journal of the Secretary of the Jesus King of All Nations Devotion: Daniel J. Lynch, Editor (Jesus King of All Nations Devotion, St. Albans, Vermont, 1993).

The Lady of All Peoples: Raoul Auclair (Les Presses Lithographiques, Lac Etchemin, Quebec, 1978).

Two Hours With Sister Lucia: Carlos Evaristo (Fatima, Portugal, 1994).

OUR LADY MEDIATRIX OF ALL GRACES

The inside back cover shows images of Our Lady Mediatrix of All Graces. All of the images show Our Lady standing on the earth as the Triumphant Queen of the World mediating to us all of the graces necessary for our salvation.

At Rue du Bac, Paris, France, Our Lady appeared to St. Catherine Labouré in 1830. She saw rays of light streaming from gems in Our Lady's fingers. Our Lady told her, "The rays are graces which I give to those who ask for them."

At Lipa, Philippines, Our Lady appeared to Terasita in 1948. She said, "I repeat to you that I am Mary, Mediatrix of All Grace."

The title "Mediatrix of All Grace" was next revealed at Amsterdam, Holland where Our Lady appeared to Eda Perleman in 1951. She said, "I come as Co-Redemptrix-Mediatrix at this time. Co-Redemptrix I was already at the Annunciation. This means that the Mother became Co-Redemptrix by the will of the Father. Tell your theologians this. Tell them moreover, that this will be the last dogma in Marian history. This picture shall prepare the way."

This picture was the model for the statue carved at Akita, Japan, where Our Lady appeared to Sister Agnes in 1973.

Similarly, an image was revealed in America in 1990 as part of the Jesus King of All Nations Devotion entitled, "Jesus Christ Mediator, Our Lady Mediatrix of All Graces." This image was drawn by the visionary whose hand was guided by Our Lady to represent her apparition. The image helps to explain the title of Our Lady Mediatrix of All Graces.

As in the Rue du Bac, Amsterdam and Akita images, the American image shows Our Lady standing on the world in front of the Cross as Co-Redemptrix and Mediatrix. Our Lady stood near the Cross (see Jn 19:25) and Jesus gave her to us and us to her. See Jn 19:26. From this holy sacrifice and Our Lady's mediation, grace and mercy come to us.

Our Lady of All Nations came to Amsterdam and identified herself as the Co-Redemptrix, Mediatrix and Advocate. She revealed that this would be the Final Marian Dogma.

Likewise, Jesus King of All Nations came to America in 1990 and said, "People must acknowledge [my Mother's] indispensable role as the Mediatrix, the Channel, of all of my grace to mankind. Only when this dogma is officially proclaimed by my Church, will I truly establish my reign on earth!"